ARTHUR E. NEWBOLD, JR., ESQ., LAVEROCK, PA.

FARM COURT

A MONOGRAPH
of the Work of
MELLOR MEIGS & HOWE

1923

REPRINTED 1991

GRAYBOOKS

BOULDER · CO

THE ARCHITECTURAL BOOK PUBLISHING CO

Paul Wenzel & Maurice Krakow

31 East 12th Street

New York

COPYRIGHT, 1923

BY

PAUL WENZEL AND MAURICE KRAKOW

NEW YORK CITY

© GRAYBOOKS · 1991

2555 55TH STREET · BOULDER, COLORADO 80301

**LIBRARY OF CONGRESS
CATALOGING-IN-PUBLICATION DATA**

Mellor, Alfred.
A Monograph of the Work of Mellor, Meigs & Howe.
p. cm.—(American Architectural Classics series)
Reprint. Originally published:
New York : Architectural Book Co., 1923.
ISBN 1-878650-01-7

1. Mellor, Meigs & Howe--Themes, motives.
2. Architecture, Domestic—Northeastern States—Themes, motives.
3. Architecture, Domestic—Middle Atlantic States--Themes, motives.
I. Meigs, Arthur. II. Howe, George, 1886-1955. III. Title. IV. Series.
NA2707.M45M45 1991
720'.92's—dc20

Printed in the United States of America

PREFACE

by

OWEN WISTER, LL. D.

Articles by

PAUL P. CRET, F. A. I. A., EDMUND B. GILCHRIST, A. I. A.,
MATLACK PRICE, ARTHUR I. MEIGS, A. I. A.,
and GEORGE HOWE, A. I. A.

INTRODUCTION
TO THE NEW EDITION
BY
DANIEL WILSON RANDLE

Pati ab igne ignem capere, si quis velit

PREFACE

B Y WHATEVER railway we journey to the Pacific coast, there is no escaping one day when it is better to read a book than to watch the scenery. To look out of a car window intelligently can add much to knowledge, even to wisdom, but not during that day through our standardized landscape of little towns, little automobiles, little box houses, bald roads, big fields, dull trees and gigantic advertisements, which blankets our continent for thousands and thousands of square miles of epic mediocrity. Every coast-bound train has to cross this, and it teaches you only what you knew already, that we are a large place, teeming with energy and sameness:—but if you left Chicago at night, it is indeed a new world that looks in at your window on the second morning, whatever train you have taken, north or south.

On such a morning once I stared fascinated at New Mexico. From the prose of yesterday, mother earth had become poetry during the dark hours. Anything of legend might fit in such a place—a caravan, extinct monsters, Don Quixote, banners carried by ghosts in armor—anything in that untamed light, beneath that tremendous sky, among those hills of mystery, so bare, so furrowed by wild chasms, so vibrating with all the savage splendors of color. Mother earth was herself a visible legend and romance so eloquent that she suggested great ancient doings and violences. Then the train stopped at a lonely junction; nothing there but water for the engine, a few passengers stretching their legs, the panting of the air-brake pump in the stillness, sun, sky, mountains—and one straight happy stroke of architecture.

What makes a house look right? Precisely what makes a piece of music sound right, a piece of verse or prose read right, or any good fabric of art of any kind—sound, words, color, substance—compel perceiving minds to give instant assent to its validity.

Did you ever ask yourself why Shakespeare's characters speak in blank verse at times and at other times in prose? Or why the rythm of DAVID COPPERFIELD is one thing in the episode of Steerforth's death and another in the Uriah Heep passages, or the Betsy Trotwood passages? Or why the orchestral texture of the MEISTERSINGER is utterly different from the texture of TRISTAN, though both are equally rich and equally Wagnerian? Or why Tennyson's ENOCH ARDEN fails to extract the full pathos inherent in the story and ends with a flat slump into the ridiculous? All such failures and successes depend upon the breach or the observance of the same law which governs architecture also.

Then what does make a house look right? Why do some seem as if they had grown naturally out of the ground they stand on, while others, some of them good enough in themselves, nevertheless bulge and glare like excrescences? Walk up Fifth Avenue along the Park. Need more be said? Were the public taste as sensitive about architecture as the public conscience is rigid as to discovered polygamy, the present library of Harvard University would no more be suffered to exist in Cambridge than a professor with a harem.

It so befell that I spent a week at that lonely junction in New Mexico, and lived in that little building. The circumstances of its growth were laid bare by two who had much to do with it. One was an old acquaintance who introduced me to the other, a lady, whose father's rare and imaginative ability had passed into her. If ever you have gone to the coast by the Santa Fé railway, you are likely to be familiar with the name of Fred Harvey, and you know his remarkable contribution towards the enjoyment of travellers. It was a creative piece of work that he did.

At this junction the Santa Fé wanted a small station hotel, a building which should combine ticket and baggage offices with kitchen, pantry, dining room, servant rooms, guest rooms, and whatever else belongs to such a place. Thus a definite, practical need, clearly understood, was the root of the matter. That a beautiful flower blossomed from this root is due to the imagination, the ideals, and the previous experience of the gardeners. As they worked out the plan in accordance with its various attendant circumstances, they never forgot the fundamental law that governed all.

The attendant circumstances were due to a few simple facts.

First, the good name that the Santa Fé had won for its meals throughout the country; hence kitchen and dining room must sustain this through their adequacy and their adjusted relation to each other—no noise, no smell while people were at table, and a dining room agreeable to the eye.   Next, the few bedrooms needed for the few ever likely to sleep here at one time, must also be comfortable and agreeable to the eye, convenient to bath rooms, and as quiet as location could make them; people must go away so well pleased that they would speak of it to fellow travellers and thus lead them to stay here instead of at the hotels in the town nineteen miles away for which they took the branch line at this point.   Furthermore, when the guests were not in their rooms, they must like what surrounded them, must feel agreeably shut in from an out-of-doors which, however picturesque, was not much like home; hence a living room must be added, and it had better have a fireplace. It might be on the front, near the tracks, but the bedrooms must be on the further side, as many of them as possible.

And lastly:

"We wanted to do something not purely commercial," explained my old acquaintance.

There again was the Santa Fé's reputation for seeing that beauty and fitness are not incompatible, and are likely to put as much money in your purse as mere ugly utility will.

So what did they do?

It was indicated by what they had done already at other points in this torrid desert of the Southwest, and that in its turn had been decided by the climate, the landscape, and the historic association—in short by exactly the very best reasons.   By chance the Spaniards came to a new world where many aspects were like those of their own country, where sun could be fierce and winds could blow very cold.   Their buildings conformed to this state of things, and consequently resembled the buildings of old Spain, which had grown through centuries of conscious or unconscious adaptation to circumstances, both in design and in material.   Following the tracks of the explorers, the Santa Fé, itself an explorer, most fitly wove the historic association into its life as a modern railway, nourishing itself with what it found in its path ready to its hand, and gaining thereby more distinction in character than any other American railway.   It might have constructed Gothic stations, or Greek temples, as well adapted as its Spanish architecture—and had it done so these would have been essentially ridiculous.   As a result of its intelligent perceptions it has created a little flower of art at the lonely junction in New Mexico, an edifice of which the outward aspect and inward arrangement are so inevitably the consequence of its purpose that they are all one thing, and cannot be separated.

EL ORTIZ—that is the name of this station hotel—is a flat, compact hacienda, basking happily in its environment. When you dine there, you sit in an artful hall where Don Quixote would have felt at home; when you sleep, it is in a room made restful by the same appropriate selection of furniture and color; in the living room you see a Mexican fire place raised from the floor, one or two old Spanish or Mexican pictures, while the very beams and supports carry out the harmony, and look seasoned with age because they are in fact nothing but sections of old telegraph poles ingeniously chosen and admirably in accord with the whole apartment.   As the scene out-of-doors is bleak, you don't look out at it, you are led to look in, at a patio with a little fountain, upon which the doors of the bed rooms and living room open.

The law by which EL ORTIZ grew lies at the root of every art and is expounded here by the architects whose work and writings follow.   It has shaped all good buildings from ancient times down to the Santa Fé railroad, and may be stated briefly thus:

Life determines the true character of any building.

Those who are concerned lest our inhabited world lose any beauty that can be saved, feel grateful to people like Messrs. Mellor, Meigs and Howe.   These architects are prophets because they preach an artistic truth in commercial times, and put it into practice: study their photographs, read their explanations, but after that, go, if you can, and see the brick and stone realities, and mark how these have developed logically according to the structural necessities of the case and the means and desires of the owner.

Life determines the true character of a building.

Given a gentleman who has a large house on a hill, with acres sufficient, and wishes to see the view not too much, and to be sunned and screened from wind in winter, to be shaded and screened from summer sultriness, to have a garden and vegetables and a farm adjacent in active operation with its various fowls and live stock—and who has the money to pay for this; or given another who needs a small house on a street with neighbors close and but a patch of ground: just as unerringly as the vital needs of a station hotel in New Mexico led straight—thanks to the competent equipment of its architects, which includes imagination—to a choice that was right, not wrong, and an expression that was good, not bad, so did the private dwellings which are photographed in this volume result in fitness and beauty, because Messrs. Mellor, Meigs and Howe, being equipped architects with imagination, obeyed the law.

And for one other reason, very important: those who were to live in the houses became collaborators with their architects.

Should you be able to visit—to take one instance—the estate where the farm was erected in direct natural relation with the house and dwelling, all of that excellence and charm has come about because the owner desired excellence and charm and took counsel how these might best be attained, given his particular case. He turned to people who could help him with their professional knowledge, which was of a widely different sort than his own. This resulted, as it should, in conferences, discussions, a process of increasing agreement, in short, it was collaboration. Not the least interesting detail to be noticed at this place is the curved ridge of the roof, not a whim but a happy outcome of the law: the slant of the land in this case was the cause.

The winds of change are blowing a gale that is thick with dust. What is happening to life in the whirling obscurity? One thing conspicuously, the crowding of charm and beauty to the wall. For this commerce is responsible. Commerce juts up from the face of the world like a host of warts, huge lumps, long welts, mills, mean rows of houses; chimneys poke into the polluted sky; commerce has stretched out a secret hand to seize the Yellowstone Park for its water power to deface and degrade a people's pleasure ground for the money in it. Is there to be nothing left upon earth but the money in it, is there to be nothing in a man's life but the money in it? What can be saved from the invasion of commercial ugliness?

Several things if we take thought; mills with a true expression growing from their structural necessities need not be an offense to the eye; but least unimpeded and most ready to our hand is the dwelling house, and no one has shown better than Messrs. Mellor, Meigs and Howe how this may keep the expiring spark of beauty alive and clothe our domestic moments with some form of grace.

OWEN WISTER.

Philadelphia, November, 1922.

INTRODUCTION TO THE NEW EDITION

AT THE FIRM'S MATURITY, Mellor, Meigs and Howe produced a body of work of such vitality and principle that it remains today a hallmark in the evolution of an American domestic architecture based on vernacular forms. Perhaps the greatest difficulty in examining this volume is that its authors elected to obscure the authorship and evolution of their work and to present it as though it were all cut from the same cloth. This is hardly the case and if one is to understand the esteem with which they were held by their contemporaries, some sorting out is in order.

In 1906, Walter Mellor and Arthur Ingersoll Meigs established a practice in their native Philadelphia that was to last until the eve of the Second World War. Mellor had been trained at Haverford College, in architecture at the University of Pennsylvania and in the office of Theophilus Chandler. A Quaker, Mellor was apparently quiet and conservative by nature and one has the feeling that in the face of his strong-willed partners he assumed a role not unlike McKim, Mead and White's William Mead who suggested his part was to run the office and to keep the other partners from "making damn fools of themselves." On the other hand, the Princeton educated Meigs brought neither professional education nor training with him. What he did contribute was his often brilliant, intuitive sense of composition, immense self-confidence and most importantly, his impeccable social connections, which when combined with those of Mellor, and later Howe, were to provide the basis for the firm's practice.

At the outset there was little in Mellor and Meigs' work that would suggest their later place in the history of American architecture. Considering their youth and lack of experience, it is perhaps understandable that they initially assumed the common and safe practice of working in historical styles. The approach was a well-mannered and conservative one, and if the earliest projects show little verve, they are nonetheless entirely competent and well-crafted. In this march through period styles, there was little in the way of a comon thread. Although the firm was later to demonstrate a well-reasoned disposition towards asymmetrical and picturesque compositions, up until about 1914 they occasionally produced projects with a formal symmetrical elegance such as the Charter Club and the rooms for Edward Browning. Mellor and Meigs' few buildings employing the local Pennsylvania colonial vernacular are fairly routine and lack the vitality that Brognard Okie and others were able to breathe into the style. Virtually from the outset, Mellor and Meigs' personal preferences were for European forms. Superficially, this might be explained by either a certain patrician state of mind, or perhaps by the fact that the colonial and Georgian work were simply too obvious. However, more importantly, the firm's best work embraced principles which precluded working in such a restrictive vocabulary. The right-angled, layered volumes of the colonial style presented few possibilities to develop the freedom of plan that characterized Mellor, Meigs & Howe's mature work. While there was a clear aesthetic in the firm's picturesque compositions, the relaxed approach to planning also had the enormous benefit of allowing for complex arrangements of highly varied spaces which could deal with the demanding topography surrounding Philadelphia. In turn, the volumes of the structures could be freely expressed on the exterior, and with a freedom of fenestration, the interior rooms could be sensitively aligned with light, principal views, and the exterior spaces into which they were often visually extended.

To the extent that Mellor and Meigs were influenced in this approach by any American precedent, it was through the work of Wilson Eyre, the elder statesman of Philadelphia domestic architecture. Eyre's highly personal synthesis of English Arts and Crafts, Queen Anne, and Shingle Style laid the groundwork for Mellor, Meigs & Howe's work, most especially in the matters of informal and picturesque planning and the melding together of styles into unified and distinctive compositions.

The first attempt by Mellor and Meigs to blend together styles was in their own offices of 1912. There the nominally Tudor exterior has a great variety of fenestration ranging in character from the quasi-industrial sash of the drafting room down to the romantic cupola, skylights, and the many-mullioned window of the Big Room, complete with its stained glass depiction of a draftsman hard at work. There is little in the building's rather austere exterior to suggest the character of the Big Room within where classical detailing was woven convincingly into the fabric of an English hall. This melding together of styles, which harkens back to Eyre, provided one of the firm's avenues of escape from the historically literal work and in time it became a comon element in their design approach. In the massing and exterior detailing of such projects as the Devereux and McIlhenney houses, the effect of this synthesis could be remarkably good. Particularly in Meigs' designs though, the quality of the interior details was sometimes far less successful and at odds with the general feel of the house. Often these disparate inclusions were defended on the basis of a re-examination of the fitness of items, but with the notable exception of metalwork, the search for improved function seldom moved beyond the adoption of an item from another style. At its worst the cumulative effect of the more whimsical elements actually diminished the whole design. At the extreme was Meigs' design for a garden room on his parents' estate (Arthur V. Meigs) which he fashioned from English, American colonial, French and Italian elements, adding a clever screen door apparently modelled on one by Harrie Lindeberg. On the exterior, this room was then juxtaposed with a classical porch and a niche for a Victorian statue which in turn were overlooked by Tudor chimneys. The result is not without charm, but in some respects its design is more suggestive of an antiquarian adding up of parts rather than the work of an architect whose details descend from a conception. Meigs may well have been the firm's most gifted designer but on occasion he indulged in an eccentric and theatrical approach to design which, it could be said, suggested his lack of formal training in architecture.

By most accounts, the entry of George Howe into the office in 1916 served to balance Meigs' most exaggerated tendencies and it is possible that Howe provided a greater focus and discipline to the firm's work. One can sense Howe's considerable abilities in his own house, High Hollow, the design for which he began as a student at the Ecole des Beaux Arts and completed before joining Mellor and Meigs. A more intellectual and formal design than Mellor and Meigs' domestic work of the same period, it also displays a number of similar interests including a conscious desire to fuse styles as well as an interest in the Shingle Style and perhaps Eyre's influence. To these influences may be added French, Italian, and Georgian references as well as Howe's characteristic playing off of symmetrical versus asymmetrical elements. Unlike the work of his future partners, however, Howe elected to fashion a synthesis which minimized detail and placed a greater emphasis on the nature of construction. To some extent High Hollow mirrors a tendency in Philadelphia domestic work that Alfred M. Githens noted in 1912 as being part of a general "Northern Tradition" which relied upon steeply pitched roofs but otherwise subordinated style and ornament to an uncontrived expression of plan and structure. According to Githens, the result was the production of an "unconscious" architecture, a term both Cret and Meigs were later to use in reference to the minor domestic architecture of northern Europe, which was to have such a profound influence on the work of Mellor, Meigs & Howe.

Soon after Howe had settled into the office, the First World War intervened and both he and Meigs found themselves serving abroad while Mellor kept the doors open in Philadelphia. The period of the war was a seminal one which seems to have generated in the partners a desire for change on a number of levels. Beyond the general sobering effect of the war, both Meigs and Howe had spent at least some of the war years in northern France and they both came to the conclusion that the region's unaffected rural architecture provided the basis for a new type of American vernacular architecture. By 1920, Meigs and Howe were in France again making detailed studies of the farms and manors of Normandy. Shortly after their return, Mellor, Meigs & Howe began to generate a distinctive vernacular architecture based on the spirit of simple volumetric forms and frankly expressed construction that they had found in France. In keeping with the rural nature of these structures the designs were worked out with restrained detailing and constructed of indigenous materials. With rare exceptions, the firm's work from 1918 on was consistently in a loose Anglo-Norman vocabulary which unlike the early eclectic work, was immediately recognizable as a distinctive Mellor, Meigs and Howe style.

Tower from the Arthur E. Newbold estate
From *An American Country House*, p.8
Mellor, Meigs & Howe, 1925

For a period following the war, the tower, often used as a juncture, was a trademark of the architects' work, as were simple wall surfaces made up of local stone with dressings of brick or roughly cast concrete. Consistent with the use of indigenous materials, the roofs were often of wood shingles. In their blending of styles, Mellor, Meigs & Howe's expressed desire was to produce an

American vernacular style. Even if the buildings were perceived as European at the time, half a century later they do appear to be a peculiarly American synthesis. The logic of the firm's intent is born out by the houses' successful integration into the older established areas of Philadelphia's Germantown and Chestnut Hill, which may form the most unified suburban areas in this country.

Residence for W. Curtis Bok near Conshohocken, PA
Mellor and Meigs, Architects

Meigs' sketch for the Bok house (1929) is typical of the firm's approach at its maturity. The plan is informal, made up of various levels, all carefully adapted to the site and the adjoining areas of the gardens. The strong interlocking volumes of the house create a clear hierarchy and produce a picturesque composition with a prominent and broken roofline punctuated by chimney stacks. The widely varying fenestration is cut out of the characteristically simple and planar walls. The lodge is essentially French, the house itself rather more English. This type of detailing contrasts sharply with the firm's equally picturesque prewar Casper Morris house. The volumes of the Bok house are simpler and more straightforward, as are the limited materials of construction. The overt historicizing of the Morris house is now largely absent, and rather than working with a single historic vocabulary, several influences are brought together. Instead of working in the manner of, say, Lutyens, one senses that they were now working in a manner distincly their own.

The Morris and Bok houses also share a sophisticated and detailed approach to the design of the entire property as well as a clear relationship between interior and exterior spaces. There are no site plans in this volume for houses prior to that of High Hollow, but after Howe's partnership the site plans of the firm's two principal designers, Howe and Meigs, are drawn out with great care. This concern may well be another of Howe's contributions, but it is also clear that the definition and development of properties was a common and necessary characteristic of the French examples that Meigs and Howe studied. Following the war, Meigs and Howe maintained an insistent control over the grounds of their projects and their commissions often involved several buildings and even the design of the gardens. In many projects the firm's emphasis seems to have been on the creation of a sheltered estate rather than on the matter of a single house. Howe was later to refer to this effort as an attempt to create a "...symbol of the fruitful soil as opposed to the hundred-acre suburban lot with its dreary monotony of lawn and landscaping." Whatever their motivation, Mellor, Meigs & Howe's ability to develop a property to insure privacy, to extend interior spaces, and to create exterior areas of differing character was one of their most significant and enduring achievements.

Even though the McCracken project was initially one of Mellor, Meigs & Howe's smallest commissions, the house and its grounds embrace the best of the firm's work. The plan of the home is a typically informal and clever one of unusual economy. The simple, picturesque forms of the building are beautifully composed and the details are in keeping. As good as the house is though, it may be on the grounds that the greatest achievement can be found. Although quite compact, the impression of the house is one of considerable size owing to the fact that the gardens and the house are inseparably one composition. The property's defining walls extend the lines of the house outwards and screen the grounds from the street and driveway (Meigs, the house's designer, was never very comfortable with "Mr. Automobile" and went to some efforts to exclude it from his compositions). The same walls continue on to introduce a fountain, support the pergola, gather the garage into the composition and then finally swell to provide the architectural focus of the belvedere. All the while the masonry drops in sections along with the grade and supports the jardinaires and the bright blue and white striped postern door which provide playful notes of color in the otherwise muted palette of materials. The actual selection and placement of the plant material was also the responsibility of the architects. For its work on the McCracken house, Mellor, Meigs & Howe received the annual medal of the Philadelphia chapter of the American Institute of Architects. The gardens were sufficiently successful that they were even published separately from the house.

The success of Mellor, Meigs & Howe's postwar buildings quickly established them as one of the preeminent firms in the country. In the age of the American tourist, the firm's widely published, informal and Europeanized version of the suburban estate found great public favor. At the same time much of the professional communtiy found a progressive quality in the simplicity, directness and inventiveness of Mellor, Meigs & Howe's work, suggesting a way to preserve the continuity of their practice, while simultaneously working their way out from beneath the cloud of criticism surrounding a design approach overly reliant on historical styles. By 1925 the Old Guard in this growing intellectual conflict awarded Mellor, Meigs & Howe the prestigious Gold Medal of the Architectural League of New York, but to many the firm had become a highly visible symbol of escapist architecture. To their detractors, the firms' progressive ideals were nothing more than an unsatisfactory compromise. Within a short time the tensions of that conflict with the modern architecture movement, were brought into the office of Mellor, Meigs & Howe and in 1929 Howe separated himself from his partners in order to become, as he put it: "...a priest of the Modern Faith." Mellor and Meigs continued on until Mellor's death in 1940 when the office was closed.

The effect of **A Monograph of the Works of Mellor, Meigs and Howe** (1923) and its sister volume on the Newbolt Estate, **An American Country House** (1925), is not difficult to assess because there is hardly a suburban community of any size in America where their offspring cannot be found. For at least a decade following its publication, the monograph served, as Howe said, as "...a handbook for the Young Romantic." The most obvious of the progeny are the innumerable cylindrical towers which were used with little discrimination as the pivots for wings of everything from palatial homes to gas stations. As often as not, these towers were accompanied by the distinctive brick diapering of High Hollow's garage and occasionally by walls of stone with window dressings and cornices of brick. Among the many towers in Mellor, Meigs & Howe's work, the entrance tower of the Newbolt Estate was the one most frequently adapted, but it is highly unlikely that anyone ever emulated its sophisticated brick roof, concrete details or the expression of its stairways as contained within the fabric of the exterior wall.

At least in popular terms, Mellor, Meigs & Howe's greatest legacy lay in the matter of strong and evocative forms and images. Their detractors also elected to focus on those things, but to suggest that is the full measure of the firm is to sell short Mellor, Meigs & Howe and their contemporaries who regarded the firm's work so highly. Despite the apparently random organization of this volume, the partners understood quite well what was their best work and they devoted the texts to them. In addition, the obvious thought and care with which the plans and details were presented makes it entirely clear the value that the architects placed in them. And if it was not always the case with details, Meigs' statement of a design approach working "up from the ground, rather than down from style" rings true and does much to belie the notion that the firm was solely preoccupied with pictorial qualities. The fact that they are handsome and easily understood buildings are hardly deficiencies. Even stripped of their dress, the best of Mellor, Meigs & Howe's projects are complex and precise works of an enduring value.

Chattanooga, Tennessee, November, 1990.

DANIEL WILSON RANDLE
Randle & Associates
1200 Mountain Creek Rd., Ste. A5
Chatanooga, TN 37405

CONTENTS

THE RESIDENCE OF CASPAR W. MORRIS, ESQ.
HAVERFORD, PENNA.

MR. MORRIS' property includes ten acres, of which about five are shown in the upper plan on page 2, and all the land slopes gently towards the south, ending with the wood and stream at the bottom. Leaving the highway, we pass through some well-established Oaks, cross the bridge, and wind along the western side of the property until we reach the Spring House where the road straightens to an axe to the Forecourt, and we find ourselves entirely shut off from the Garden by the wall connecting the Spring House with the Porch. This line of demarcation between the north and south continues to the east of the house, where another wall extends to the eastern boundary line, thereby keeping the Entrance Drive, Forecourt, Garage, and Services completely separate from the Garden, Porch, Terrace and Orchard. The Forecourt is surrounded on two sides with buildings, while the other two sides are bounded by a Ha-Ha wall capped with a hemlock hedge, and made necessary by digging the Forecourt into the slope of the hill.

In design, the house builds up from low elements at either end to a high accent in the middle, starting with the porch at the west, which is one story, through the transitional element of the Sleeping Porch to that part of the house which is over the Living Room, and is a story and a half high; on to the two and a half story wing over the Dining Room and Services, and finally, back to the low Garage, the northern end of which is below the natural grade of the land.

Entering the Front Door we pass through a low and narrow Hall to the South Terrace, or if we turn and enter the Living Room, we find ourselves upon another axe looking through the Bay Window across a Pool which forms the center of interest of the whole outside scheme.

The Porch is situated at a short distance from the house in order to darken none of the rooms, and provided with ornamental wrought-iron grilles to the north, and brick openings to the east, in order to attract any Summer breeze, while the connection between it and the house takes one past the Pool and under the Sleeping Porch, in the design of which an effort has been made to bring beauty out of necessity. Porch, Passage, Sleeping Porch and House are all mirrored in the Pool— an ancient device in architecture.

Details are perhaps more easily understood from photographs and drawings than from a written description, but to enumerate some of the more important ones, the Forecourt is paved with small cobble stones of about the size of a hen's egg, laid in a bed of cement and divided into panels with bricks; all exterior woodwork about the Porches and half-timbered work is of solid Oak, oiled and allowed to weather to a light, brownish gray, while the timber work shown on the south side is structural, the overhang being supported by a large truss shown on Page 7; the walls are built of a combination of brick and hollow tile covered with yellowish gray plaster, while the brick about the windows is specially moulded to an intricate detail, as shown on Page 12; the roof is of split shingles, the gutters, down-spouts and flèche over the Archway are of copper, and the weather vane at the top of the corner chimney of the Forecourt was suggested by the thought that ascending and descending cats are not an impossibility on the roof of any house and these two turn with the wind on top of the chimney and tell the Owner where the wind sets by a dial on the ceiling of the Den below.

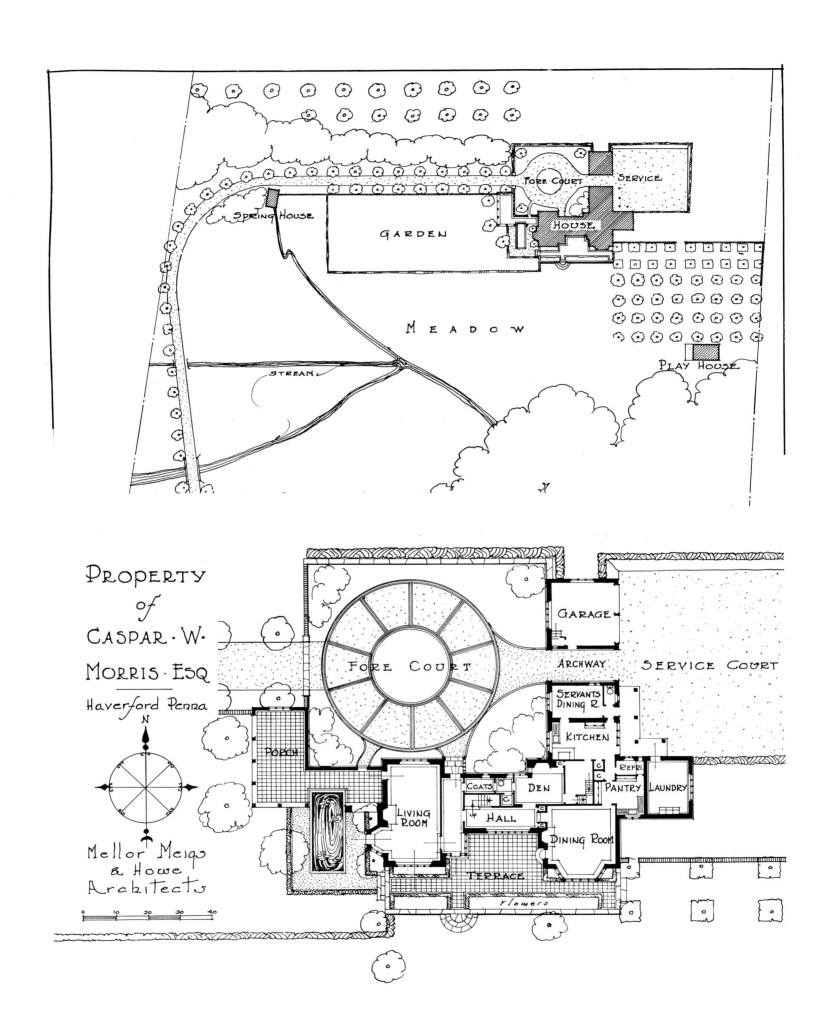

PROPERTY
of
CASPAR·W·
MORRIS·ESQ

Haverford Penna

Mellor Meigs
& Howe
Architects

CASPAR W. MORRIS, ESQ., HAVERFORD, PA.

1916

FORECOURT

CASPAR W. MORRIS, ESQ., HAVERFORD, PA.

1916

GARAGE AND ARCHWAY FROM DRIVE

SOUTH FRONT

CASPAR W. MORRIS, ESQ., HAVERFORD, PA.

1916

IRON GRILLES IN PORCH

PORCH FROM ARCHWAY

POOL FROM PORCH

DETAIL OF SOUTH FRONT AND TERRACE

CASPAR W. MORRIS, ESQ., HAVERFORD, PA.

1916

SLEEPING PORCH

CASPAR W. MORRIS, ESQ., HAVERFORD, PA.

1916

DETAIL OF SOUTH FRONT

LIVING ROOM

ENTRANCE HALL

SOUTH PASSAGE

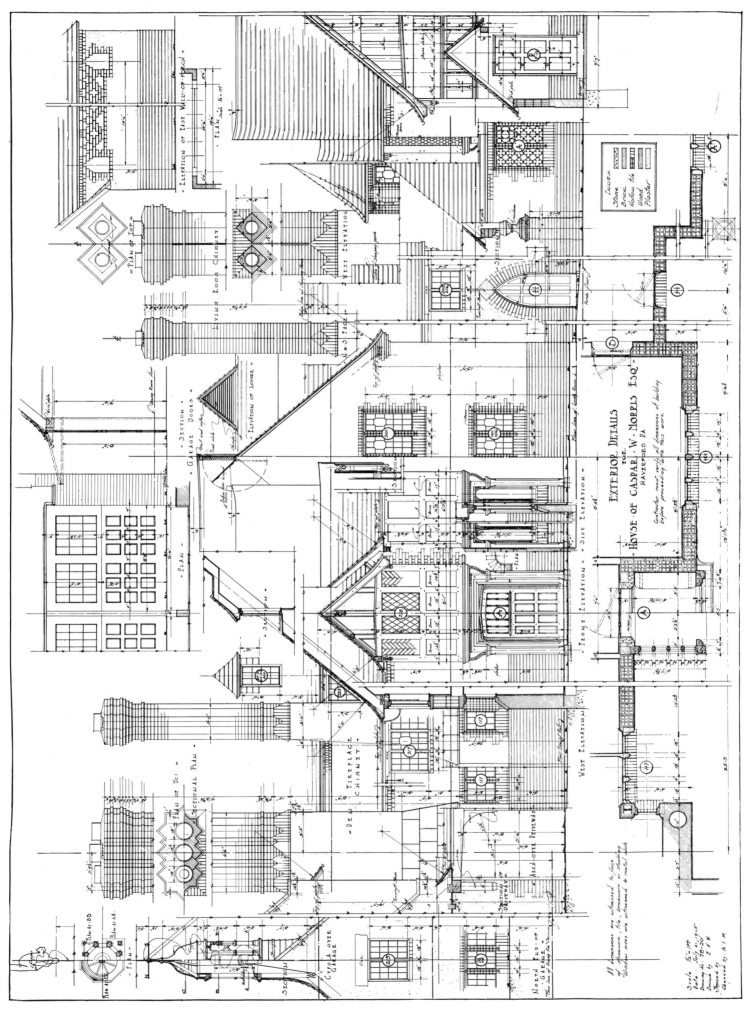

EXTERIOR DETAILS (NORTH SIDE)

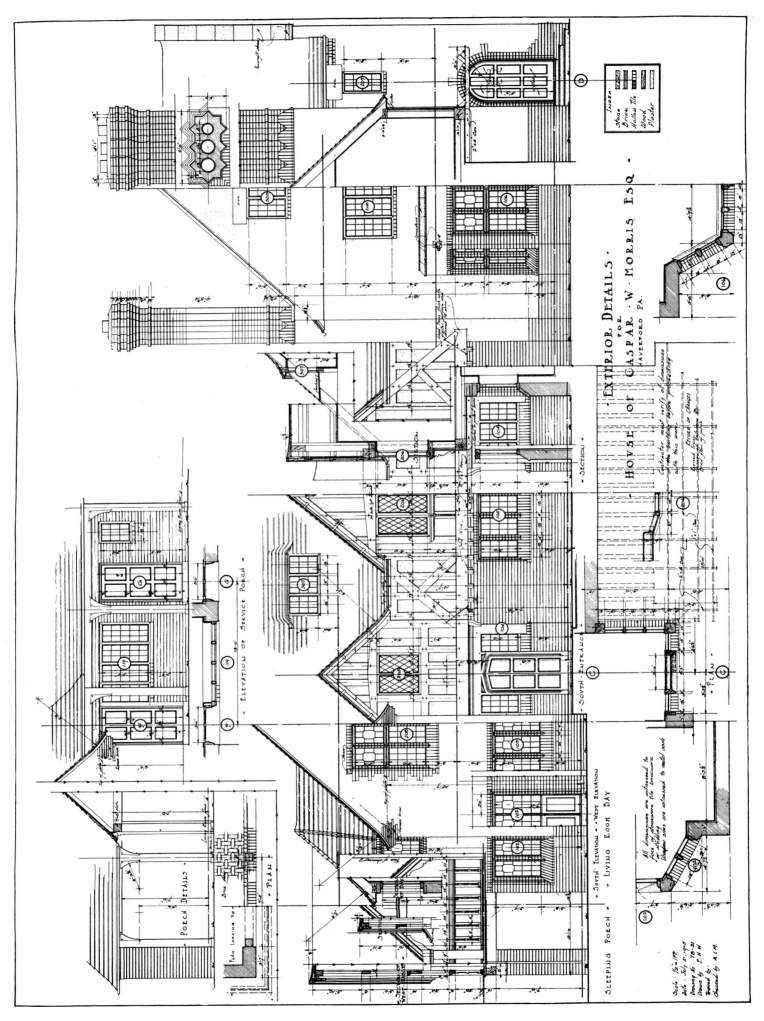

EXTERIOR DETAILS (SOUTH SIDE)

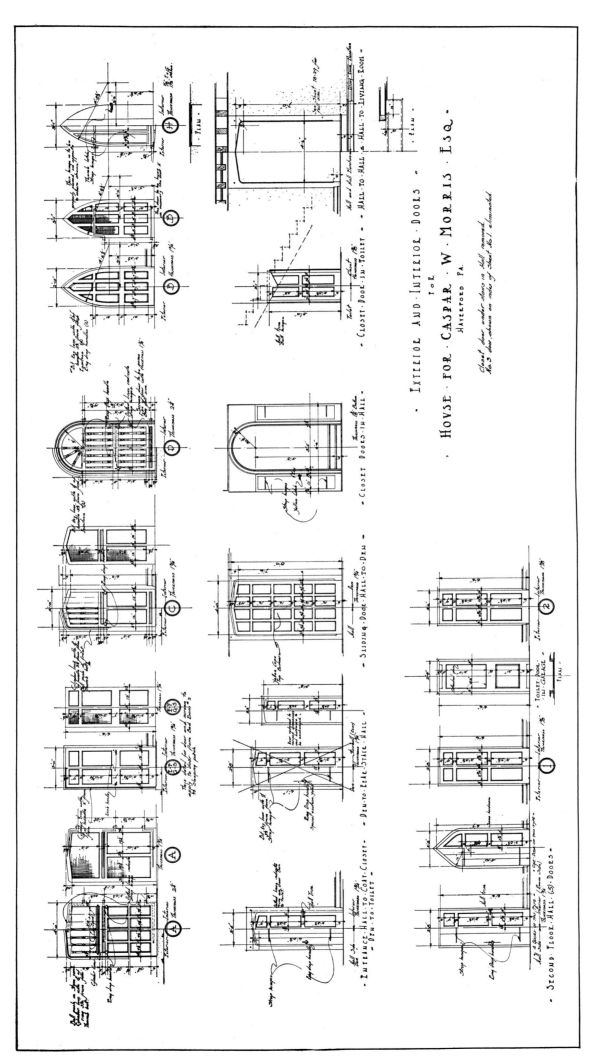

DOORS

11

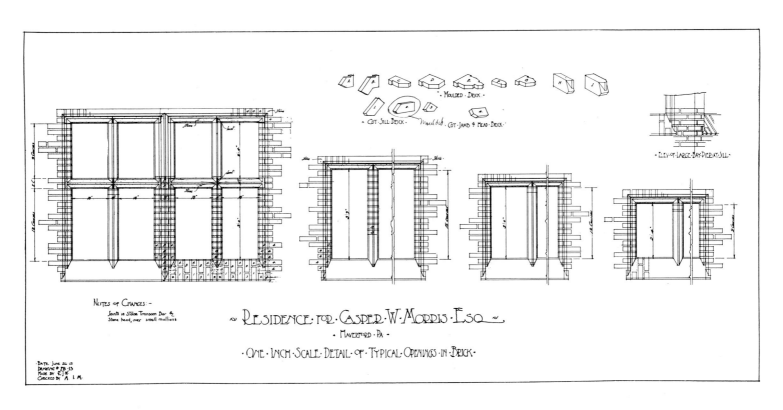

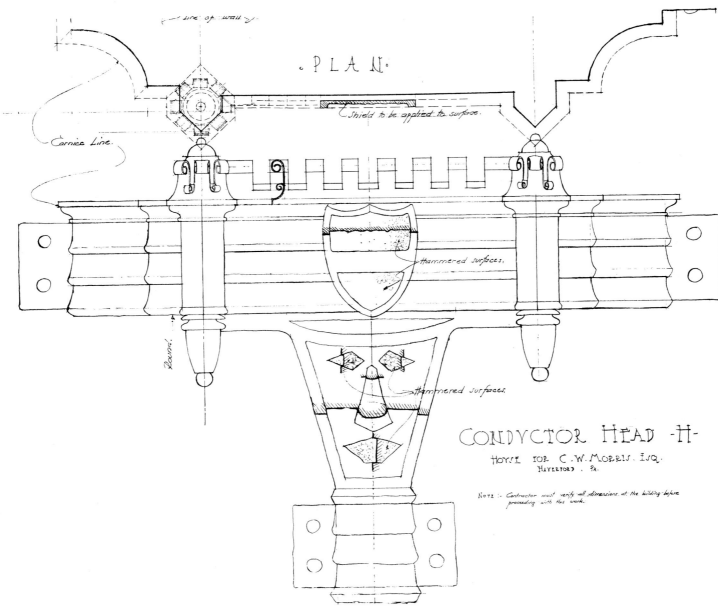

BRICK DETAILS AND CONDUCTOR HEAD

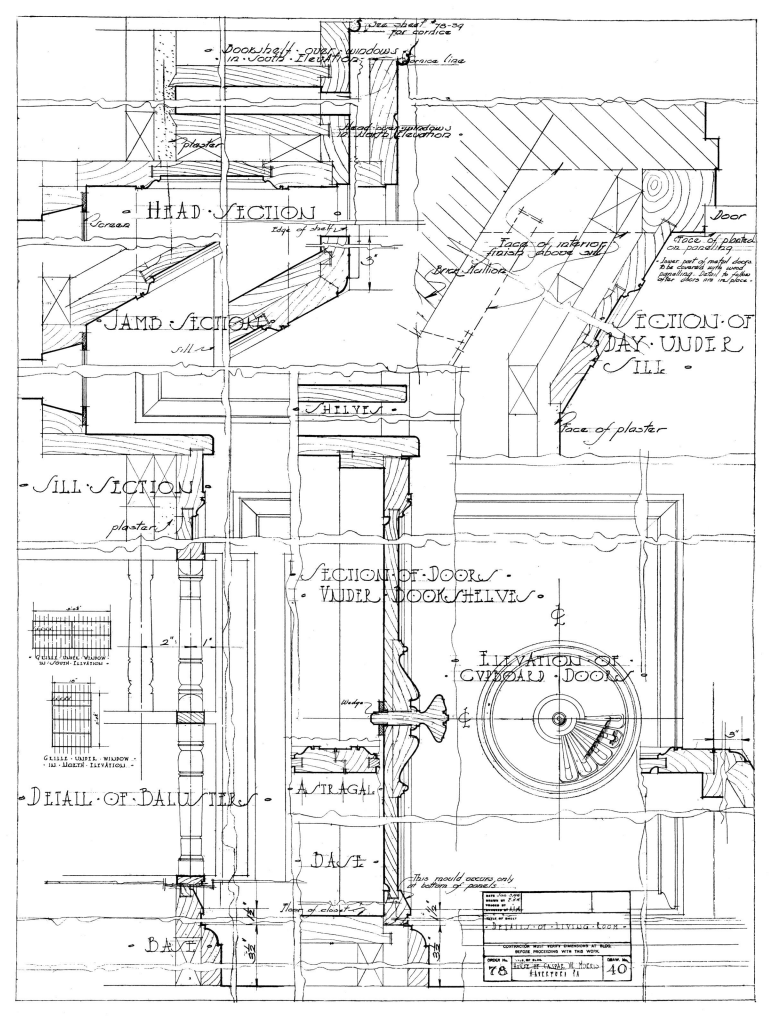

DETAILS OF LIVING ROOM

HIGH HOLLOW, THE PROPERTY OF GEORGE HOWE, ESQ.
CHESTNUT HILL, PHILADELPHIA

REPRINTED FROM THE AUGUST, 1920, ISSUE OF THE ARCHITECTURAL RECORD

FROM the terrace the lindens are outlined on a background of hills that one might suppose remote from all cities and human turmoil. Two other sides are enclosed by the woods rising at the rear of the grounds and the third by the house. The shadow of a giant oak, a bench against a hedge of hornbeam, and that same feeling of peace that reminds one of cloisters in Italy or of an eighteenth century garden in a sleepy provincial town of Touraine. Is there a better place to read? I wish I had had there that volume of Edgar Allen Poe, in which he develops his views on landscape gardening, as he most irreverently calls it. Some passages would find their illustration right around. That one, for instance, in which he claims the superiority of the artificial style (which we nowadays call formal) over the natural style. ". . . . The artificial style has as many varieties as there are different tastes to gratify. It has a certain relation to the various styles of buildings. There are stately avenues and retirements of Versailles; Italian terraces; and a various mixed old English style, which bears some relation to the domestic Gothic or English Elizabethan architecture. Whatever may be said against the abuses of the artificial landscape-gardening, a mixture of pure art in a garden scene adds to it a great beauty. This is partly pleasing to the eye, by the show of order and design, and partly moral. A terrace, with an old moss-covered balustrade, calls up at once to the eye the fair forms that have passed there in other days. . . . Of course everything depends on the selection of a spot with capabilities."

Poe would have liked this setting of the house; a setting which is so skilfully selected that one forgets that it has been created in the last two or three years. It seems just as integral a part of the hill as the terraces and houses of Amalfi are of the cliff over the bay. The greatest achievement of art is to make itself inconspicuous. The terrace wall curves along to follow the contours, just as do those stone walls which retain the scarce loam of the vineyards. The service wing seems to have used an old foundation, as those houses rest on the old fortified gates of a city.

To find so perfect an example of a complete group, and above all of a group where the gardening, the architecture, the smallest details are exactly fitted to the importance and the character of the whole, is far from common. Look at the plan. There is almost no rectangular form; nothing seems to force itself on the natural conditions, and nevertheless there is everywhere that "mixture of pure art" of Poe. It has that beauty of the village street that follows the capricious lines of a path of old, so superior to the relentless gridiron of our surveyors. It is picturesque without affectation.

For those who have followed the development of the art of Messrs. Mellor, Meigs and Howe, its most interesting feature has been precisely this progressive mastering of the charm, of the unconscious beauty of the minor domestic architecture of Europe. In each successive work there is a progress in the elimination of the "draughtsman picturesque" and a step toward that simplicity that is achieved only by the very few. There is less and less of what could be called the bric-a-brac of architectural repertory, and in each case a stronger affirmation of individuality.

In this particular instance they had, it is true, the privilege of choosing a most remarkable site, for the owner is also the designer and a member of the firm. That is luck, but some one has said with reason that opportunity knocks only at the door of those who know how to receive it. With a property of moderate size, within the city limits, the boundaries of a public park have been used to such advantage as to incorporate the park woods in the composition. In going over the grounds, one does not realize the limited extent of the estate, neither does one wish for other conditions. There is no need for an apology.

Poe, in the same essay I quoted, "The Domain of Arnheim," develops a theory that might at first seem to disagree with the location selected for the house: "The taste of all the architects I have ever known leads them, for the sake of 'prospect,' to put up buildings on hill-tops. The error is obvious. Grandeur in any of its moods fatigues, depresses. For the occasional scene nothing can be better, for the constant view nothing worse. And, in the constant view, the most objectionable phase of grandeur is that of extent; the worse phase of extent, that of distance. It is at war with the sentiment and with the sense of *seclusion*—the sentiment and sense which we seek to humor in 'retiring to the country.'"

The latter part of the passage will explain why, while agreeing with these principles, I did not feel that the location was condemned by the first part. There is a vista, from the entrance and from the principal rooms of this house. However, this vista is naturally such as not to give the feeling of being lost in space, as does an extended view. The photographs can hardly show the converging lines of the valley, forming a sort of wooded amphitheatre with a narrow opening in the main axis toward the bluish line of a more distant hill. There is the same feeling of seclusion from the world as is given by the main perspective in the Villa d'Este, framed by high trees, and leading the eye to one focus, instead of offering too many subjects to the observer. And it is this division of interest that causes fatigue, much more than mere distance. By eliminating it, or by selecting a natural site free from it, the impression of calm is at once restored.

The illustrations accompanying these notes would make any comments superfluous, were it not for the fact that there are two groups of buildings that no photographic reproduction has ever adequately succeeded in representing. They are those buildings in which color plays an important part, and those that derive their merit from successful proportions more than from decorative details. This house belongs to both.

Of a very moderate size, it gives, however, a feeling of spaciousness quite remarkable; and this is due, above all, to a most careful study of the proportion of the rooms. All mouldings, ornaments, recesses, all those things that are commonly called "architectural trimmings," have been eliminated. The authors of an excellent book on interior decoration have written: "Proportion is the good-breeding of architecture." Here is indeed an example of that "noblesse," that distinctive elegance achieved only by a highly developed culture.

And when I speak of proportion, I have not in mind those tabulated recipes of a Vignola. The only use of classical forms is the Palladian motive in the entrance hall. In the rooms, the walls rise without a break from the floor to the smooth ceiling. Outside, the masonry, with its vari-colored stone, enhanced by lines of brick, is the only decoration; but the fine outline of the roof crowns the whole building and gives to it a dignity which takes us far from the involved tricks of suburban country houses.

These walls, built shortly before the war, seem to be old. A careful selection of their material (an old quarry was reopened to secure it) and a still more interesting workmanship have contributed to this result. As I noted before, the house and its garden seem to have been always there. I have no doubt that the owner had from the very first month of occupancy this same feeling. And yet a remarkable fact is that the house is quite free from imitation of historic precedents in its details. Were not the phrase "modern art" somewhat discredited for having been a cloak to a multitude of sins, I would see here a very typical example of what modern art ought to be: a logical continuation of the best traditions. It is as free from archaeological imitation as it is devoid of a pretentious striving for originality. There again the good-breeding asserts itself.

As someone who had recently visted it told me: "It does not look like a Philadelphia house." It is a distinct departure from the usual types—some of them of great merit—which for the last twenty years have been the fashion in the neighborhood. In few words, it has personality. Look at the very bold treatment of iron balconies on the garden façade; at the most ingenious arrangement of the stairway; and note the omission of those well known details which come at their assigned place, like certain rhymes in amateurish poetry. Everywhere one finds an expression of forms that seem to have been created for that particular place, and without effort.

No doubt many clients would be disappointed by their inability to tack a "style" label to any portion of it. This consideration had no weight in the case, for, as I have said, the architect is also the owner. The living room is neither Elizabethan nor Jacobean; the dining room is not Louis XVI. They are both designed with a true sense of the decorative effect produced by the nature of the floor, the color and texture of the walls, and, above all, by their proportion. They attempt to be nothing more than a setting for the furniture, some tapestries and a few paintings, and with the true conception of a setting—that it must be nothing but a background for the players. There are interiors, of course, not complying with this rule, which are masterpieces. Bare of furniture, the rooms of the Doges' Palace or the "Grands Apartements" of Versailles are still beautiful. They belong, however, to that kind of stately rooms which have an entirely different function from those in a moderate sized house; besides, they were intended to receive a very small amount of furniture, as we learn from the contemporary engravings. For a different program must be found a different solution, and we find here a new proof of the unerring artistic sense of Messrs. Mellor, Meigs and Howe. They have resisted the temptation to design an interior like an exterior elevation, which has to stand on its own merits or with the scant assistance of planting at its base.

There is much to say on the skill shown in the placing of furniture and hangings in the rooms. This furniture, collected by the owner with the same good taste characterizing his professional work, has been used in the composition of the rooms exactly as any integral part of the building. It is not often that the architect has this opportunity, in spite of the fact that he is better prepared than anybody to do it. The grouping of seats around a cabinet, the placing of a bronze or marble of the right size and color over this cabinet, the selection of the tapestry that will set off the whole, the right height for the hanging of a painting in a panel, all this is designing with various elements and requires an eye trained to the sense of proportion, the combination of color, and the juxtaposition of volumes, that is to say, the esthetic part of architectural studies. It does not imply that the architect has necessarily to be the adviser in the selection of the pieces of furniture that he may be called upon to place in the rooms. He may advise on the best grouping of elements already belonging to his client in the same way that the landscape architect makes use of the natural conditions of a site and of shrubs which are not made to order but grown in nurseries.

As noted above, an important element of the work of Messrs. Mellor, Meigs and Howe is the color. Its value is entirely lost in photographs. On the exterior, the vari-colored stone work to which I have referred, enhanced by its lines of brick, is composed of natural seam-faced stones of dark buff, brown and reddish hues. The woodwork is of a dull blue. The combination has the merit of having a value approximating the deep green of the trees around, and thus preventing the house from "standing out" from its background too sharply.

Inside, the scheme selected is no less remarkable. The key for the living room was given by the fine tapestries hanging on the walls. The floor is made of Enfield tiles of a grayish yellow with borders of a dull blue. These same blue tiles turn around the windows and the fireplace; the ceiling and walls are painted a gray-yellow, which sets off the old pieces of furniture. The entrance hall has been composed around the vista seen between the columns when one enters the front door. Everything was then subordinated to this neutral note of color. A pavement of black and white marble and the gray-buff walls form an appropriate frame to enhance the distant landscape, in the way that a cardboard mount strengthens the delicate tone of a water color.

The dining room was evidently designed for a painted frieze of the seventeenth century, faded like an old pastel, that occupies the upper part of the walls, which are divided in very simple panels and painted an ivory tone. Around the fireplace a border of Italian tiles, with yellow and blue ornaments on a white background, is the only other note of color. The floor is made of marble tiles. In the oval room, a most ingenious scheme was used for the floor. A rough cement, stained with oil, becomes interesting by the contrast of a border of green tiles surrounding four medallions of Enfield mosaics of a wonderful color and design. This very new and appropriate treatment has great possibilities and opens a large field for the use of this material.

One can judge by these four very different treatments of the pavement of the care given to every detail of the whole. These floors may seem to the reader to have received an elaboration and a quality of material out of keeping with the wall treatment, but again I find that the architects are right in spite of the usual practice. When we enter a room, or stay in it, our field of vision, unless we make a special point of studying the architectural treatment, grasps the furniture nearest to us, a small portion of the lower part of the walls, and a large expanse of floor. When the floor is an uninteresting area of hardwood, or a plain carpet, we feel the necessity of relieving it by placing here and there the rich color and pattern of Oriental rugs. This is somewhat of a makeshift, for the rugs seldom agree either in character or color with the rest of the decoration, which is thus thrown out of balance. One can easily see the advantage of using a pavement designed for the room. It is not an extravagance, as might be objected, if one considers the cost of fine rugs, and it adds a sort of substantiality to the general treatment that carpets or rugs are unable to supply.

The photographs illustrating these notes have been selected by the architects with two ends in view. One is to secure a logical presentation of their work, in the sequence that the visitor of the house is most likely to follow. By reference to the plan, it is always easy to understand what is shown in the picture and to gain a complete understanding of the arrangements. The other aim is to show only those pictures that give the true aspect of the house and grounds, that is, to eliminate views taken from distant stations, or pictures showing aspects that the visitor does not really perceive. The optic angle of a camera is quite different from our field of vision; the result is that many photographs show much more than we can really see at one glance. By limiting the field covered by a picture, the result approximates much more closely the real impression received by a visitor. It is hoped that the very complete set given here will allow a fair study of this hillside house.

It is a study well worth the time given to it. I will, for instance, point out in the general layout, besides the complete adaptation of the plan to natural conditions that was mentioned above, the very interesting solution of the division of spaces. It is not simply a pleasant combination of garden-architecture forms; it has also the quality of the well-planned industrial plant where each process of fabrication is in the right relation to the preceding and succeeding processes. There are some spaces for sitting (the upper terrace and the lower garden); spaces for walking (the green walk, the pleached walk); spaces for working; and each of these in the proper place and with the special character it deserves. The terrace, for instance, is the logical extension outdoors of the living room. The green walk takes one through ever-changing aspects.

The greatest pleasure will be found in discovering in these features, which at first seem to have been adopted without thought, a clever adaptation of the great principles of design; in realizing that this architecture, which owes so little to precedents, is true to the best traditions of art; in finding the soul of our art instead of the cast-off clothing of former time.

It would be an interesting study to analyze the methods by which the architects secure in modern work the charm of these old European country houses, so unpretentious that they seem without architectural merit to the casual observer, even though he be impressed by a peculiar quality not found in more elaborate buildings. Superficial students dismiss the whole question by ascribing this subtle quality they cannot otherwise explain to the fact that the buildings are old. Age has indeed a mellowing influence on buildings which cannot be overestimated. It gives the roofs those undulating surfaces which blend their lines with those of the distant hills. It stains the walls and clothes them with ivy. It brings additions and alterations to the original scheme that are a new and unexpected note. It is not, however, the sole cause that makes the tourist deem worthy of a snapshot a farm courtyard and its rambling buildings, a manor in Normandy or a peasant's house in an Italian village. There are other reasons, and in their research Messrs. Mellor, Meigs and Howe have gone much further than most of the men I know.

PAUL P. CRET.

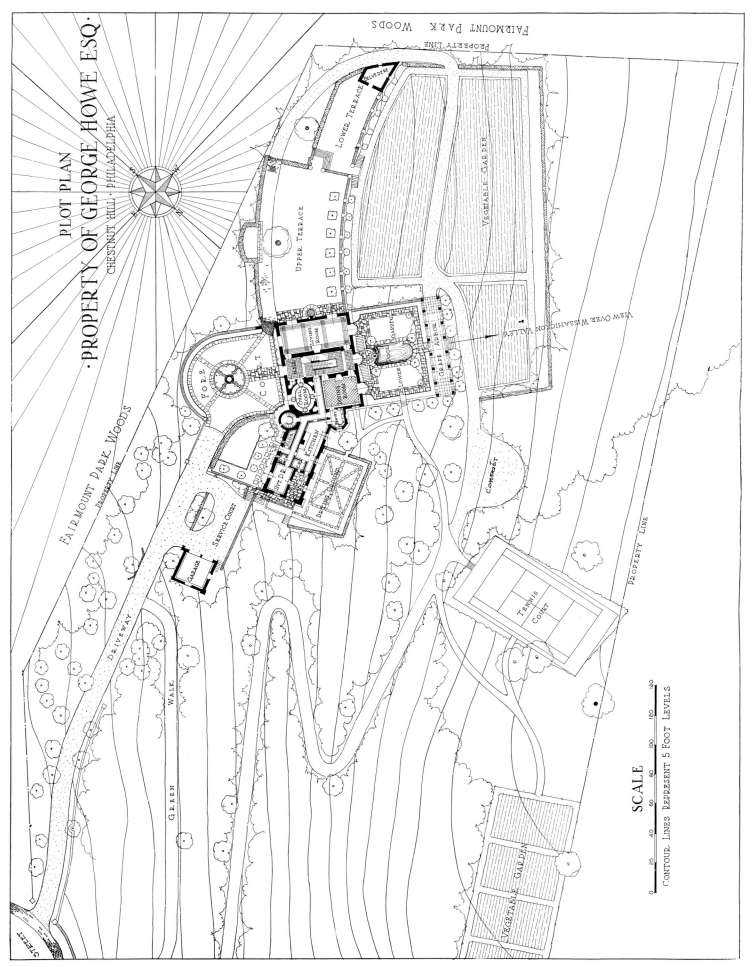

PLOT PLAN

·PROPERTY OF GEORGE HOWE ESQ.·

CHESTNUT HILL · PHILADELPHIA

FAIRMOUNT PARK WOODS

FAIRMOUNT PARK WOODS

PROPERTY LINE

PROPERTY LINE

PROPERTY LINE

PROPERTY LINE

LOWER TERRACE

BELVEDERE

UPPER TERRACE

VEGETABLE GARDEN

VIEW OVER WISSAHICKON VALLEY

GRAPE ARBOR

FORE COURT

SERVICE COURT

GARAGE

DRIVEWAY

GREEN WALK

STREET

COMPOST

TENNIS COURT

VEGETABLE GARDEN

PLAN

SCALE

0 20 40 60 80 100 120 140

CONTOUR LINES REPRESENT 5 FOOT LEVELS

HOUSE FROM DRIVEWAY

FORECOURT AND WOODS

LIVING ROOM FROM FORECOURT

FORECOURT FROM LIVING ROOM

VIEW FROM UPPER TERRACE

HOUSE FROM LOWER TERRACE

ENTRANCE AND TOWER FROM GATE OF UPPER TERRACE

GEORGE HOWE, ESQ., CHESTNUT HILL, PHILA.

1914

ENTRANCE DOOR FROM FORECOURT

HOUSE FROM THE GREEN WALK

GEORGE HOWE, ESQ., CHESTNUT HILL, PHILA.

1914

STAIR HALL LOOKING TOWARDS ENTRANCE

STAIR HALL FROM ENTRANCE DOOR

DETAIL OF LIVING ROOM FIREPLACE

GEORGE HOWE, ESQ., CHESTNUT HILL, PHILA.

1914

DETAIL OF LIVING ROOM

LIVING ROOM LOOKING TOWARDS FORECOURT

25

DINING ROOM

VIEW FROM LIVING ROOM

THE STUDY

HOUSE FROM BELOW TERRACE

LOWER GARDEN AND HILLS FROM STAIR HALL

HOUSE FROM LOWER GARDEN

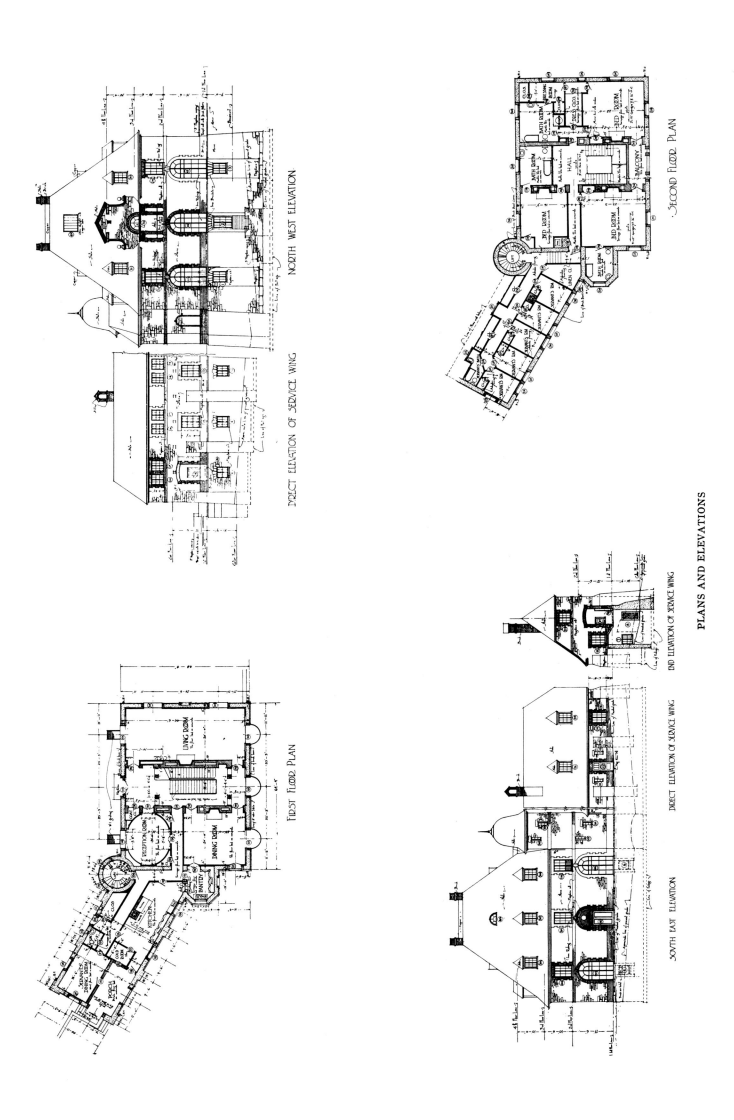

PLANS AND ELEVATIONS

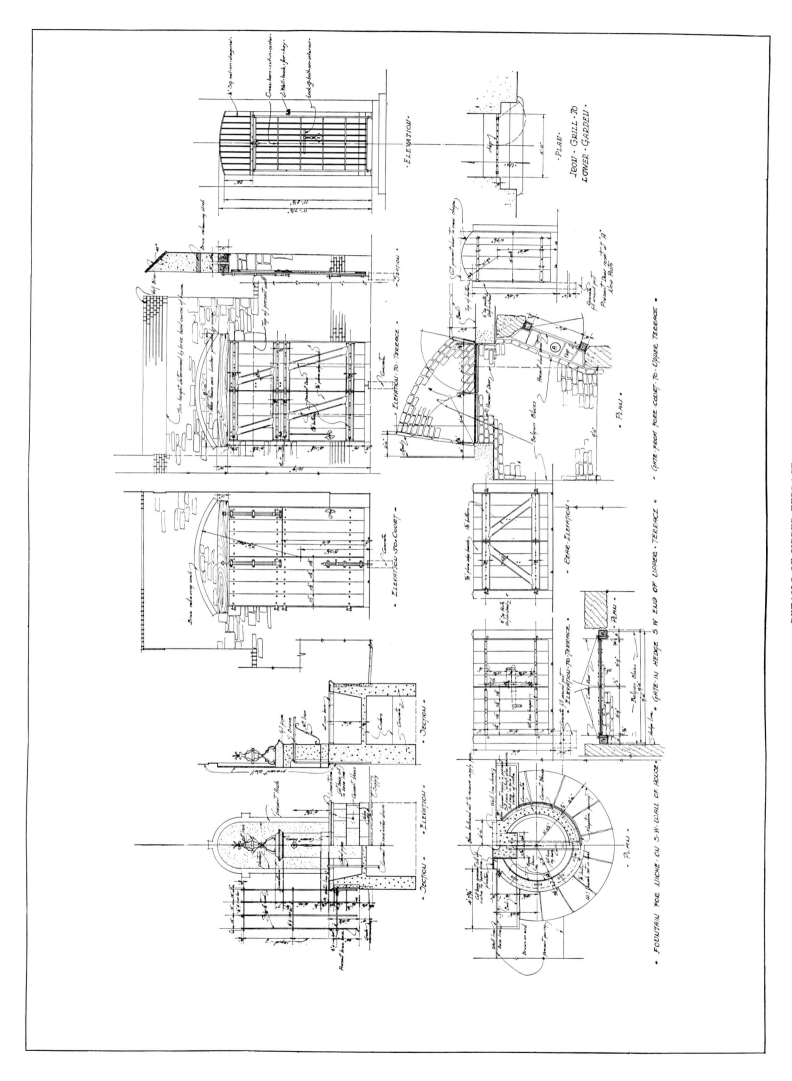

DETAILS OF UPPER TERRACE

(Executed too recently to be photographed)

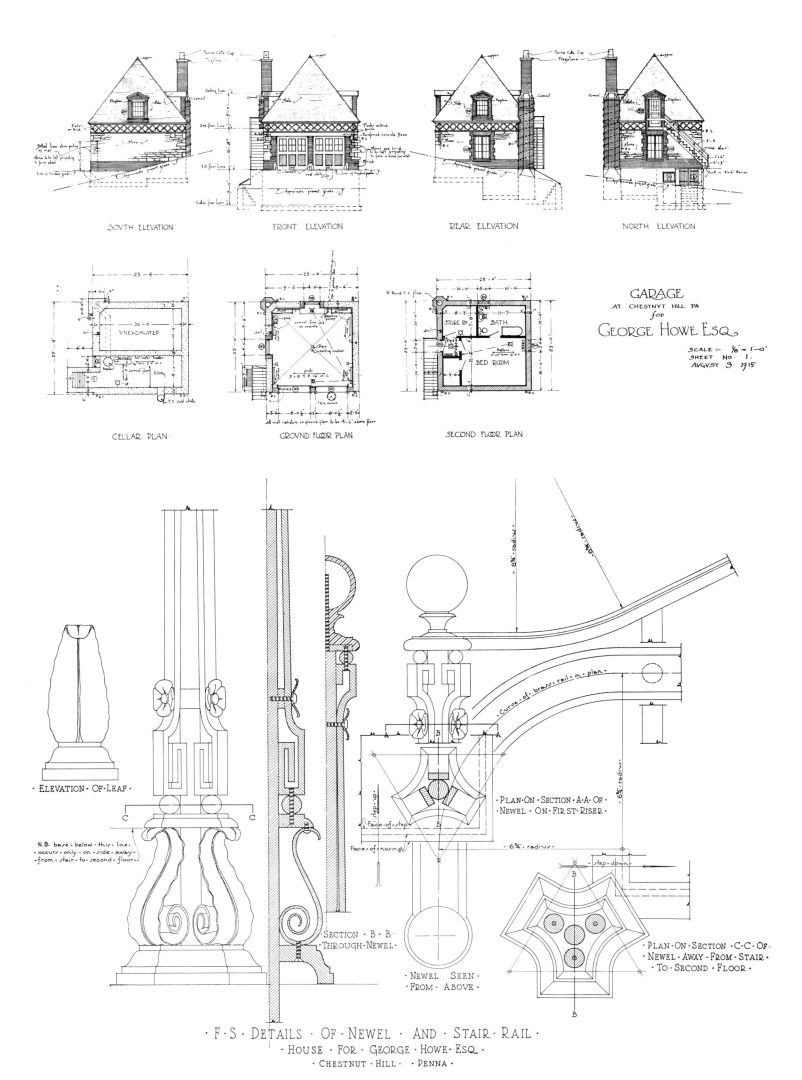

SOVTH ELEVATION   FRONT ELEVATION   REAR ELEVATION   NORTH ELEVATION

CELLAR PLAN   GROVND FLOOR PLAN   SECOND FLOOR PLAN

GARAGE
AT CHESTNVT HILL PA
for
GEORGE HOWE ESQ

SCALE ⅛ = 1'-0"
SHEET NO. 1.
AVGVST 3 1915

· ELEVATION · OF · LEAF ·

N.B. base below this line
occurs only on side away
from stair to second floor.

· SECTION · B · B ·
THROUGH · NEWEL ·

· NEWEL · SEEN ·
· FROM · ABOVE ·

· PLAN · ON · SECTION · A · A · OF ·
· NEWEL · ON · FIRST · RISER ·

· PLAN · ON · SECTION · C · C · OF ·
· NEWEL · AWAY · FROM · STAIR ·
· TO · SECOND · FLOOR ·

· F · S · DETAILS · OF · NEWEL · AND · STAIR · RAIL ·
· HOUSE · FOR · GEORGE · HOWE · ESQ ·
· CHESTNVT · HILL · PENNA ·

GARAGE AND STAIR DETAILS

THE RESIDENCE OF FRANCIS S. McILHENNY, ESQ.
CHESTNUT HILL, PHILADELPHIA

Reprinted from the October 1919 Issue of "The Architectural Forum"

IN THE consideration of the problems involved in the design for the house of Mr. Francis S. McIlhenny two principal basic considerations were at once apparent. First, that the house was to be built upon a hill, and second, that the hill sloped towards the northeast, and that the outlook was directly to the north. These two points formed the root and foundation for the whole design. Regarding the question of orientation, it was decided that the solution of the problem lay in planning the house in such a way that the principal rooms would look out to the southeast, and this necessitated the creation of the parterre at that point. By this arrangement the living room, the hall and the writing room, on the first floor, and the owner's bedroom and the other two principal bedrooms on the second floor, obtained this valuable exposure. The question of view, to a large extent, was subordinated, but, by the location of the dining room, the bay looks directly at the view, the living room has two windows facing it, and the porch is so placed that it commands both the parterre and the view. In order to get the sun also into the dining room, the sunken garden was created, and while practical considerations make this a necessity, it brought about, as is almost universally the case, when such considerations are successfully handled, one of the pleasantest features of the design.

In fact, this process was followed throughout, and if the finished product has any merit at all, it is entirely due to the plan being born from its situation, and the elevations and outbuildings following as a logical sequence from the parti originally assumed. Of all elements of design, this seems to be the most important, and the one that, if faithfully, frankly and logically followed, produces in the end the most successful results. If the parti suits the ground, if the house is set at the right level, and if it is set in such a way, with regard to the points of the compass, that the sun gets into the principal rooms, that the places in which one lives outside are both cool in summer and warm in winter; everything else in the design seems to fall into its natural place and takes care of itself. The designer can find ready to his hand an answer to almost any question which may arise, if what he started with was right and suitable and if he can treat what he does afterwards with taste and a sense of the beautiful.

The functioning of a place of this kind is of the utmost importance. The property is about four acres in extent, and of this scarcely two are available for buildings, namely, those which show upon the plan, while the balance of the property extends to the northeast and further down the slope.

The two ramps at either side of the main gates to the Forecourt, which show on the plan, but not in the plates, are an interesting illustration of beauty growing out of necessity. They form a pleasant feature and, although built before the greenhouse, they now constitute the only connection between the garden functions of the place and that part of it which lies to the southeast of the sunken road.

Such matters, too often forgotten, show the importance of thinking and designing beforehand, while it is frequently the case that the owner takes the position that he wants from the architect only the design of a house; that the matter of the functioning of his house, and the functioning of the various things that go with it, are considerations entirely apart from the service to be expected from the architect, — the result being in so many instances that the outbuildings are located in a haphazard fashion and, frequently, in wrong and inaccessible places.

With regard to planting, practically all that shown on the plan has been done through co-operation between the owner and the architect, and here again, an opportunity exists which is too often neglected. When the designer creates blank spaces which exist in his mind as covered with vines, climbing roses, espalier fruit trees, or any other such pleasant appurtenances belonging to a country house, and those spaces are treated entirely differently and unsympathetically by an owner quite unconscious of the designer's conception, and aiming at a different object, thoroughly unsatisfactory results may be expected from the two opposing forces.

The levels were such that, in order to get the main first floor at an elevation equal to that of the parterre, formed by cutting out on one side and filling in on the other, this first floor level had to be set five feet lower than the level of the forecourt, thus necessitating the entrance loggia with its flight of steps leading from the front door to the actual entrance to the hall.

It would be quite impossible to classify the house as belonging to any style. Certainly the plan is English in feeling, inasmuch as it is both broken up and irregular, wandering about the property in a haphazard fashion, with no attempt at formality, considerations of orientation having taken precedence at every decision.

Fenestration of the house could be considered either French or Italian, though certain features—such as the entrance loggia—are quite slavishly Italian. As for French influence, — the bricks around the windows and the free use of brick as a color motive around the cornice and various other places might be said to be taken from the French, while the form of the roof is perhaps nearer French than anything else, but the fact of its being covered with shingles puts in an American touch.

An attempt has been made in presenting this house in the plates to arrange them serially, so that one is taken from the front—beginning at the entrance from the highway, through the forecourt, showing various views of the elements there, passing through the gate to the Garden, and after numerous views of it, returning to the interior of the house, and finally out of the Dining Room and back to the Sunken Garden.

One year elapsed between the broaching of the original proposition for designing this house and the breaking of ground for its construction. Another year elapsed while it was building, two more until the building of the Green House, and it was not until the Spring of 1922 that the Garden was built—six years after the first beginnings.

The owner having come to the very wise decision that he expects to live in the house for the rest of his natural life, proceeds slowly with the new features of the place, thereby getting his amusement as he goes along, and conditions such as these are undoubtedly ideal from the standpoint of the architect.

A new experiment was tried with regard to the treatment of the plaster walls in the porch and entrance loggia. The walls in these two places were sand-finish, and it was felt that color was desirable. In the loggia, three main colors were decided upon,— yellow, brown and blue, all colors being very strong, and the brown about the tone of Spanish leather. Taking these three colors in three separate pots, the walls were covered in irregular shaped blocks, so that when they were first finished, they looked more like a ship that had been camouflaged than anything else. The colors were blended together by putting blue over the brown, brown over the blue, and both blue and brown over the yellow. A very successful result was thus obtained in which the color starts with yellow at the bottom, blending into brown half way up, and ending in a very rich blue on the vaulted ceiling, though there is no part of the surface that is all one color, as the three colors vary and intermingle throughout the entire surface.

The porch walls and ceiling are treated similarly except that the ceiling is a strong yellow, while the walls graduate up from yellow, through a pink orange, into a violet at the top.

The most careful study has been put upon the Garden and the matter of landscape architecture is perhaps as much neglected in this country and in the present times, as it is important, as a general idea seems to exist that, compared to the house, it is relatively unimportant, and that the house being finished, there is little else to do.

Design is quite as important in landscape work as it is in architecture, except that it is more evanescent, more difficult to apprehend, and more rare.

Masses of growing things, whether they be trees, hedges or an open lawn, bear a relation to each other quite as important as the relation between the masses of architecture proper, and to suppose that the harmony, or lack of it, existing between the width of a terrace and the wall back of it, the size of an open space and the height of the features surrounding it, or any such elements of proportion — in short, design —- are unimportant, is a most profound error.

In this Garden, the effort was made to keep it simple in mass, and rich in unobtrusive detail, flower beds being almost eliminated. Color exists in the architecture itself and in the brick and gravel walks; the level green carpet of the Parterre, the trees and the woods form the background, and the flowers in pots and jars are the accents, but it should be taken into consideration that it is less than a year old and awaits the quality that age never fails to bring.

It is interesting to note that a free use of concrete has been made and that all concrete was cast on the job. All this work was done by the carpenter, the mason, and the common labor, and every baluster shown came from two moulds cut out with a gouge from solid blocks of wood. The color of the concrete is similar to that of Indiana Limestone, and the surfaces were untouched after the removal of the moulds, thus obtaining a sympathetic texture without effort or expense.

One porch can be habitable only at one time during the day; in this case there is a place to go both morning and afternoon, as the porch in connection with the house becomes shady at about three o'clock in the afternoon, and the Belvedere affords a capital place in which to spend a hot summer morning, overhung as it is with well-established trees and looking out over the principal view of the property.

The circulation around the Parterre as expressed by the paths has been carefully studied to be continuous, and to afford both variety and interest. The Parterre is an element open to the northeast and closed on the other three sides with features of different heights; the house to the northwest, the serpentine wall, capped with pleached trees, to the southwest and the Belvedere, Lion Fountain and Tool House, backed by the woods to the southeast. This circulation runs completely around, beginning with the main terrace of the house, through the porch, along the open side, across the steps of the Belvedere, thence around the Lion Fountain to the Tool House, and finally back along the serpentine wall. The upper walk through the alley of pleached trees is an additional variation.

To sum up, there were two principal decisions taken before the design was really started, which have created many of the most important features of the house, and the influence of which was so strong that it seems to extend into almost all the details. These were first, the orientation and, second, the level at which the main floor of the house was set.

The entire arrangement of the rooms, the placing of the forecourt, service court, parterre, vegetable garden, greenhouse and garden, resulted from the former, while the sunken garden, entrance loggia, the feature of the garden itself, and the garden gate with its steps and pool, all followed in logical sequence from the latter. Whether the results are good or bad is open to question, but certain it is that, from the standpoint of the designer, much more pleasure and benefit may be derived from the planning of a house, up from the ground, rather than down from a style.

ARTHUR I. MEIGS.

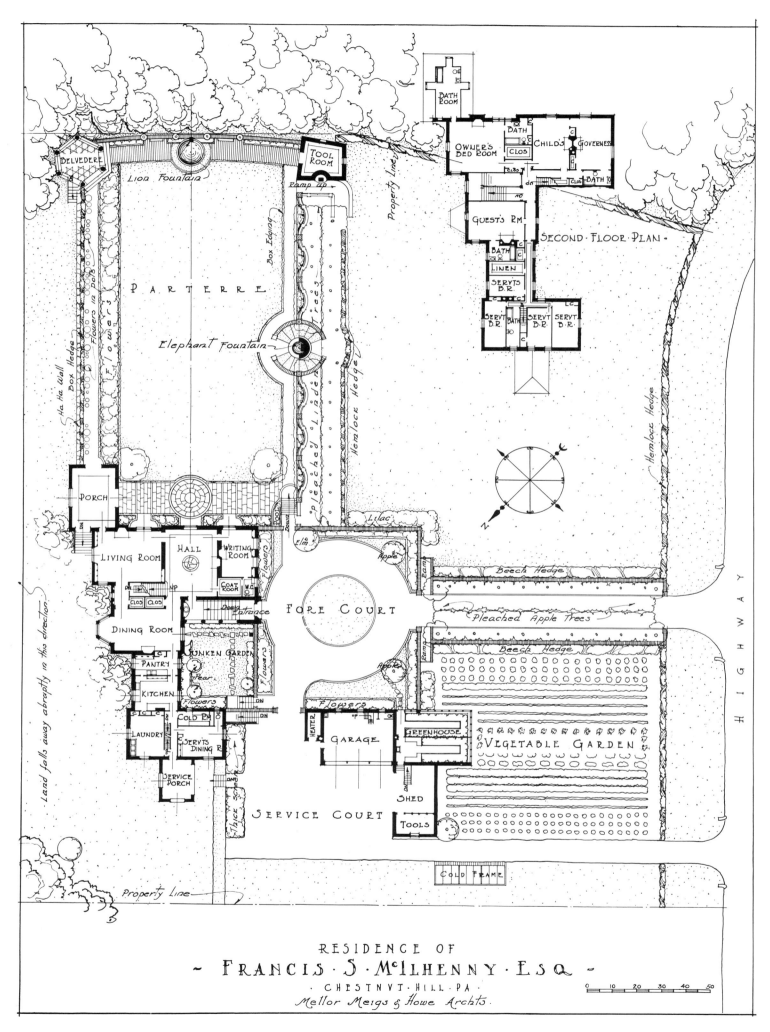

RESIDENCE OF
~ FRANCIS · S · McILHENNY · ESQ ~
· CHESTNVT · HILL · PA ·
Mellor Meigs & Howe Archts

PLAN

FRANCIS S. McILHENNY, ESQ., CHESTNUT HILL, PHILA.

1918

HOUSE FROM HIGHWAY

GENERAL VIEW

GARAGE AND GREENHOUSE

FRANCIS S. McILHENNY, ESQ., CHESTNUT HILL, PHILA.

1918

SUNKEN GARDEN

HOUSE FROM SERVICE COURT

FRANCIS S. McILHENNY, ESQ., CHESTNUT HILL, PHILA.

1918

ENTRANCE FRONT

DETAIL OF FRONT DOOR

GRAPES AND GRILLES

FRANCIS S. McILHENNY, ESQ., CHESTNUT HILL, PHILA.

1918

ENTRANCE LOGGIA

BACK OF ELEPHANT FOUNTAIN

GARDEN LOGGIA FROM UPPER WALK

FRANCIS S. McILHENNY, ESQ., CHESTNUT HILL, PHILA.

1918

LION FOUNTAIN AND BELVEDERE

HOUSE FROM UPPER WALK

FRANCIS S. McILHENNY, ESQ., CHESTNUT HILL, PHILA.

1918

GARDEN FROM HALL

LION FOUNTAIN AGAINST THE WOODS

HOUSE FROM LOWER WALK

GARDEN GATE FROM FORECOURT

GARDEN GATE FROM PARTERRE

TOOL HOUSE

ELEPHANT FOUNTAIN

TOOL HOUSE WITH DANAID

WISTARIA TRELLIS

STAIR END OF HALL

FROM WRITING ROOM TO PARLOR

MAIN STAIR LANDING

HALL MANTEL

WRITING ROOM

PARLOR FIREPLACE

BELVEDERE FROM PARLOR

PARLOR

SUNKEN GARDEN FROM DINING ROOM

DINING ROOM BAY

DINING ROOM

STEPS INTO SUNKEN GARDEN

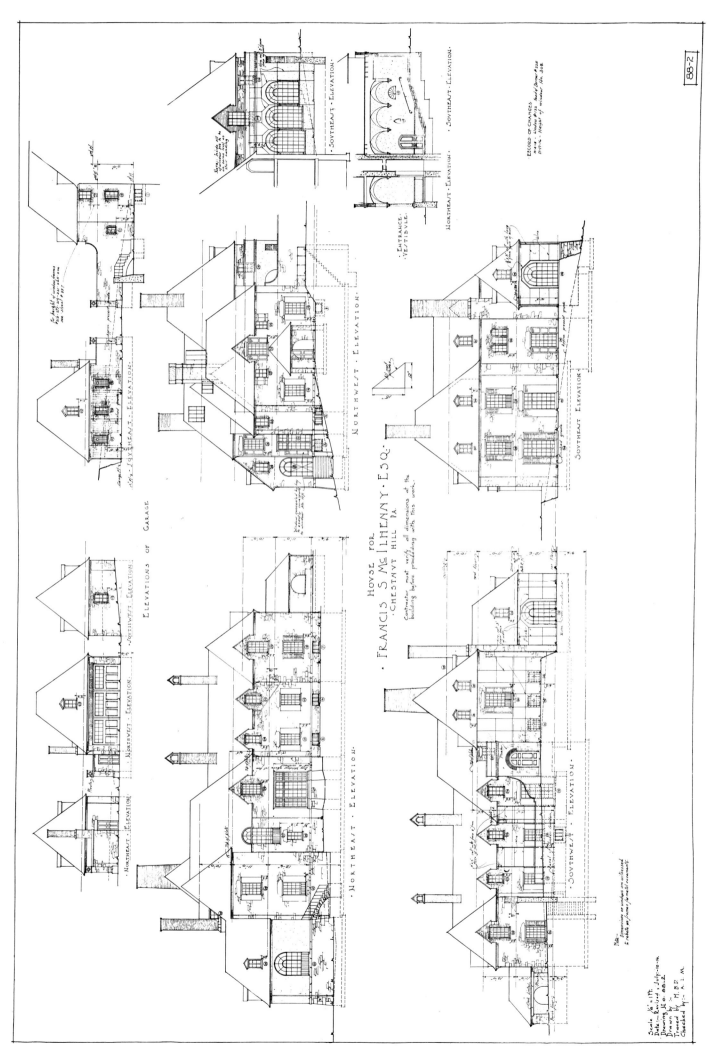

ELEVATIONS

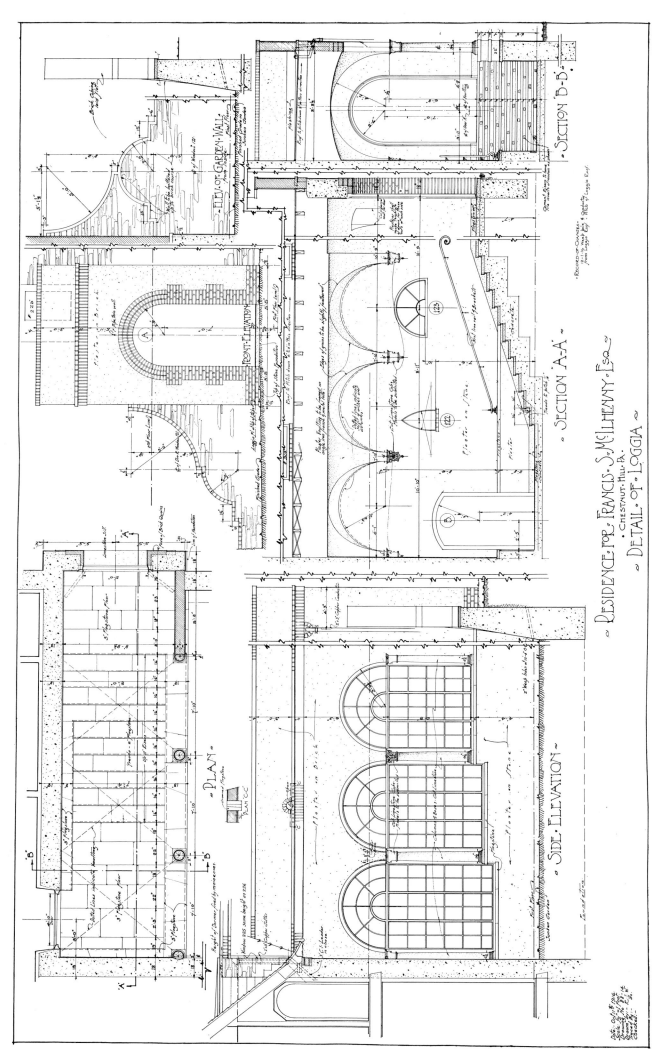

ENTRANCE LOGGIA

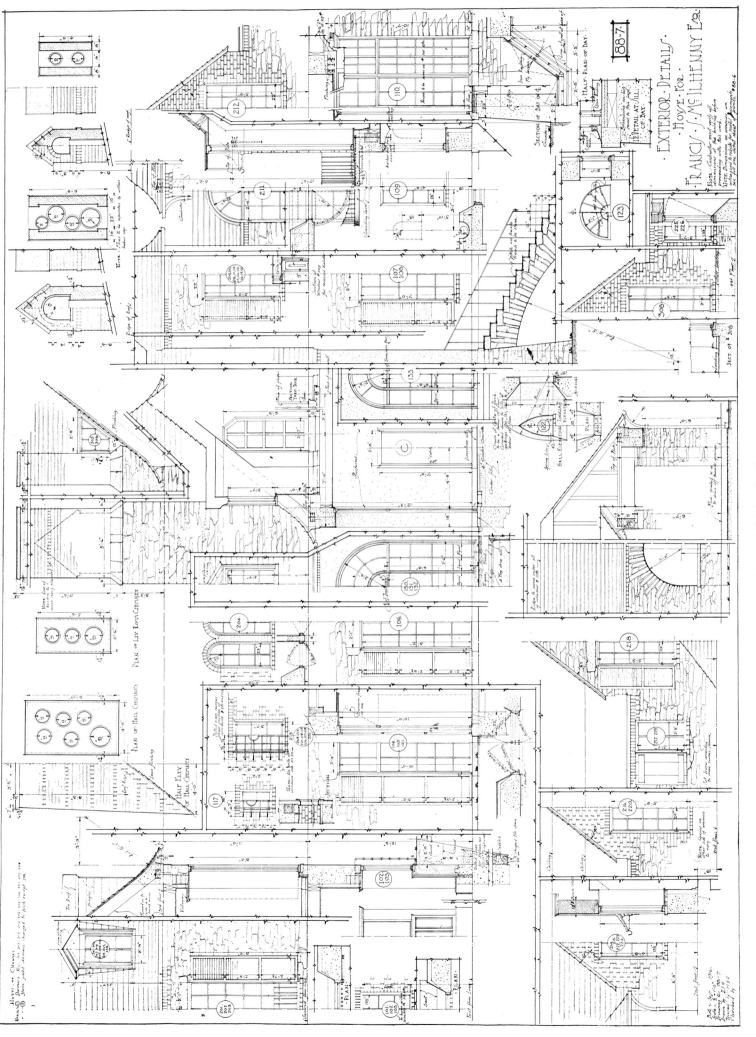

EXTERIOR DETAILS

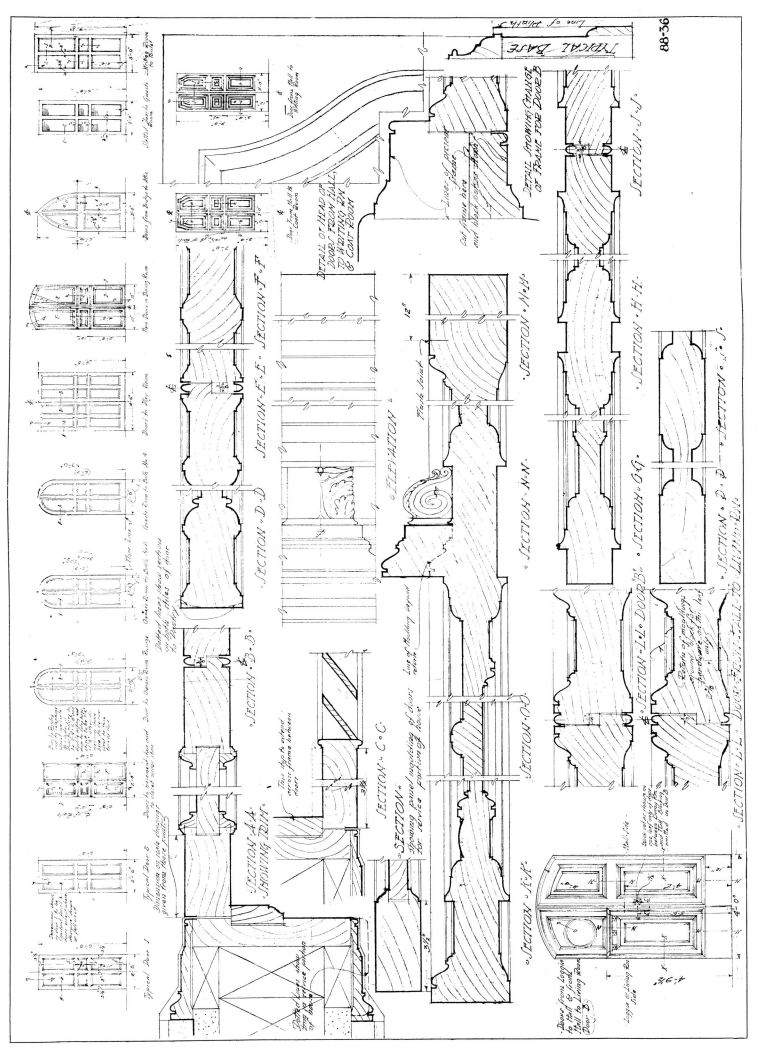

DOOR DETAILS

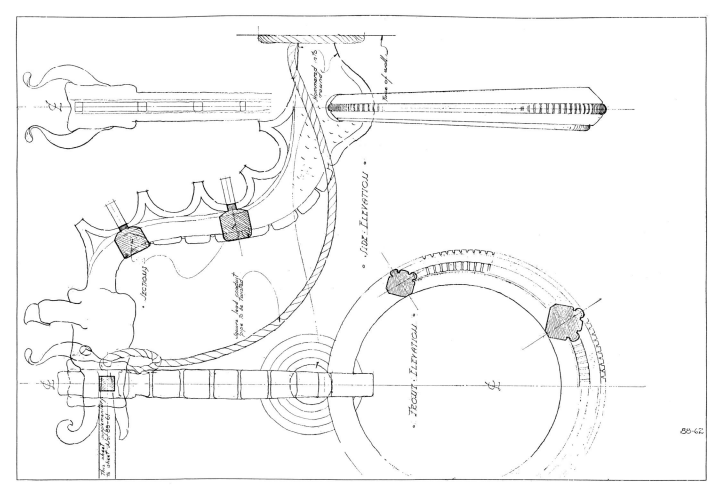

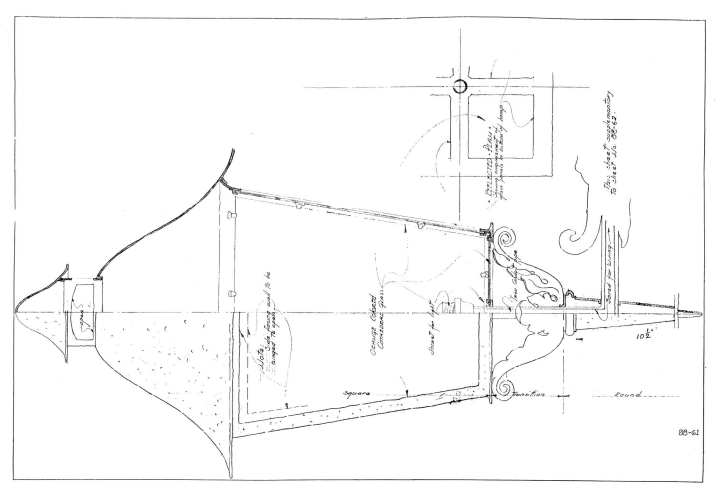

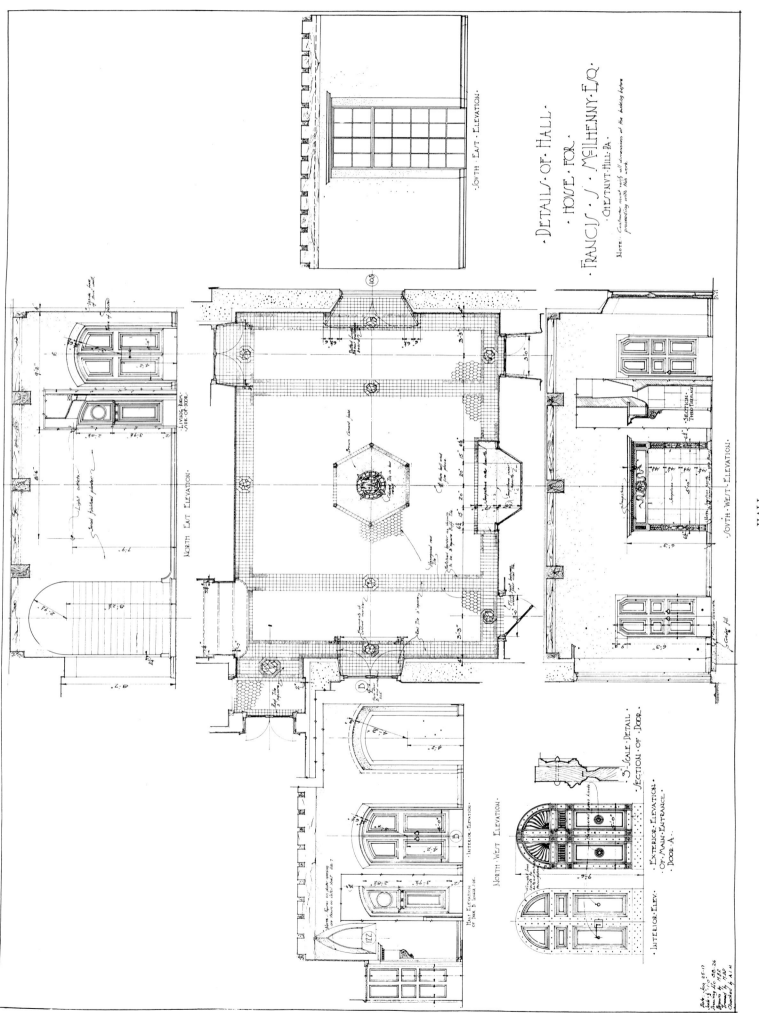

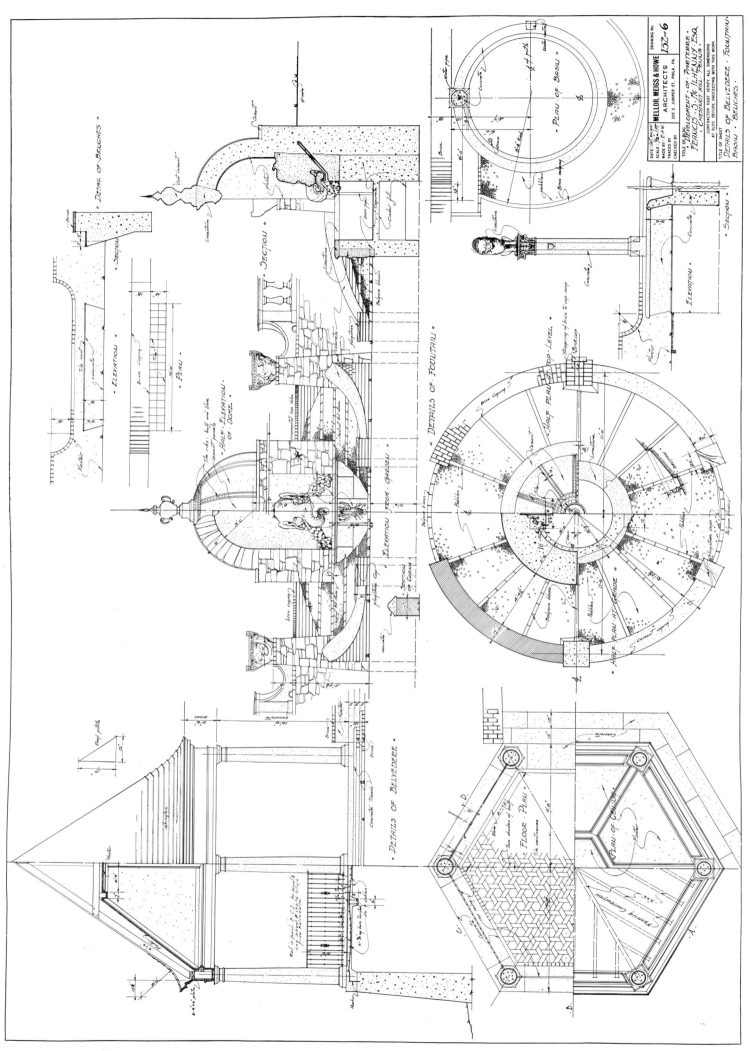

BELVEDERE AND FOUNTAINS

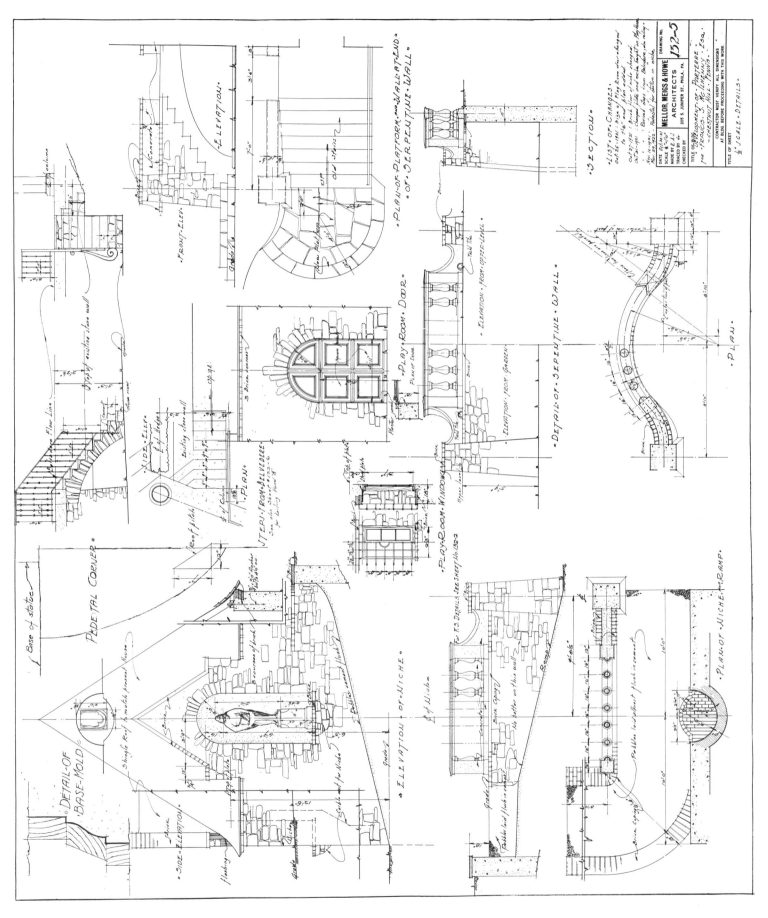

TOOL HOUSE AND SERPENTINE WALL

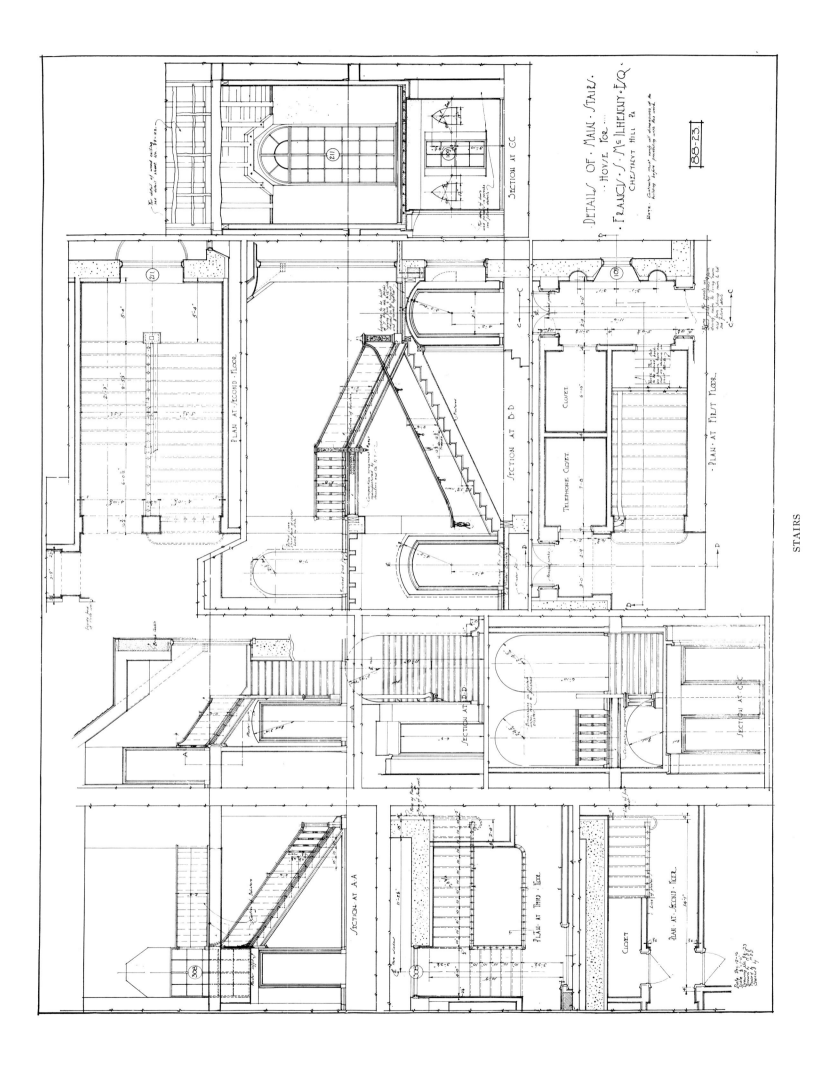

STAIRS

THE HOUSE OF ROBERT T. McCRACKEN, ESQ.
GERMANTOWN

REPRINTED FROM THE SEPT. 1921 ISSUE OF ARTS AND DECORATION

IT IS by no means difficult to assign a reason for the conspicuous scarcity of examples of good small houses.

Most small houses do not come from the designs of architects, but are usually a builder's unskillful compromise between several houses seen in book or magazine illustrations, or they are copied as nearly as possible after other houses of similar cost in a certain locality. It is by no means surprising that this kind of small house, especially if it is built on speculation, to sell to any chance purchaser, should lack architectural qualities.

Everything in a small house counts tremendously, and if the whole thing, from the study of the plan, through to the detailing and supervision of the work, is done in a mechanical and, usually, a scant manner, the result can only be regarded as "building"—not as architecture. When an architect is engaged to design a small house, several things usually occur, some of them inevitable, others arising more indirectly from the nature of the problem.

It is inevitable, for instance, that one real mistake in a small house, whether in its planning or in its design, will ruin the whole effect, while it might be of virtually no significance in a large house. From the initial condition of its smallness, the small house usually means a limited expenditure and rigid architectural economy. Moreover, the small house client usually worries more than the prospective builder of a large house, and his worries do not aid the architect in creating a fine and unhampered piece of work. They insist upon working into the house more whims and restrictions, more commands and interdictions, often contradictory, than the design of one small house can sustain and still retain true character.

Often the cost restriction hampers both client and architect in creating a beautiful small house: both would be in accord if there were a little more money available. So the house is finished as a fabric of compromises, expressing neither the client's taste or individuality nor the architect's ability. The architect who sets out with a high standard for a small house must be gifted not only with strictly architectural ability, but, even more, with ingenuity and resourcefulness, with the knack of making the most of every inch and every dollar.

The charm of a small house, its livable qualities, its picturesque values, do not depend upon expenditure. A thousand dollars, one way or another, on some one item of material or labor, may, of course, make a very noticeable difference, but the skillful architect is the one who can come the nearest to satisfying his professional conscience and realizing his client's aspirations within an allotted sum of money.

Concessions on both sides are often necessary—neither architect nor client can afford to be autocratic in planning a small house—and harmony in the architect-client relationship, which should always be a real friendship, will smooth out many difficulties and achieve many triumphs, as will be seen later.

The mistake of many small houses takes the form either of attempting too much or of attempting too little. A small house should never attempt to be a large one, but on the other hand it need not be stupid or unbeautiful. A small house is neither a portion of a large house, nor a miniature version of a large house: its problem is a special one, and it is a distinct kind of house.

In its broadest terms the problem of successfully designing a small house resolves itself into devising and effecting a maximum of practicality, beauty and individuality within a fixed cost limit. The entire plan, including every closet and door, and all the permanent equipment, must be practical, for there is virtually no margin for error. The element of beauty will come first from sheer design, and second from the suitability and inherent qualities of the materials used, and from the technique with which these are used. The element of individuality will be measured by the success with which the architect understands his client's temperament and expresses it, the expression mingled, perhaps, with some elements of the architects' individuality in design and technique.

In order to achieve these things, every element of planning and designing must be utilized to its utmost. Briefly, I would say that the main aims of the architect who is trying to create a successful small house would be to develop with a maximum effectiveness the layout of the site, the floor plans of the house, its pictorial qualities in design, the choice of materials and any and all ingenious devices which will add practical and individual character to the whole house.

Much, in the first place, can be done with the site, meaning the entire grounds. The small house need not be a forlorn little box, crying its smallness to every passer-by. Terraces, walls, hedges, gates and skillful planting can impart the essential element of design to the whole premises, and just as every bit of space in the floor plan can, with sufficient study, be utilized, so can every bit of space in the grounds be made a part of the complete design. Upon the floor plans, obviously, must depend the practical success of the house. They are the source of the pictorial aspect of the problem, and yet they must be carefully considered from the first, and developed hand in hand with the pictorial effect.

The beautiful little house which, inside, is inconvenient, ill-arranged and impractical is no better, architecturally, than the efficiently and well-planned house which stands up, uncompromisingly box-like, from a bare, clipped lawn.

Given a good plan, the pictorial aspect of the small house is highly important. The beauty of a small house, *as a picture*, may make its size such a minor question, by comparison, that the beauty is all that is seen or remembered, and the owner will receive a certain kind of sincere envy from many owners of large and burdensome houses.

In the matter of materials—skill and imagination in selection will not only aid the pictorial aspect of the house, but will impart also another small house essential—*character*. Lack of character is the distinguishing demerit of the preponderant majority of small houses.

The foregoing brief survey of the general conditions of small house design, both ideal and actual, is intended as an aid in the appreciation of this exceptional small house in Germantown. It possesses such ideal qualities in every essential respect that a detailed exploration of the whole premises cannot fail to hold much of inspiration and practical suggestion to all who are thus far interested.

The house, with its long dimension parallel with the road, seems to occupy but little of a property frontage of a hundred feet. To the right an unnoticeable driveway leads back to a service court and a garage, both of which are entirely invisible from the garden. From the highway, then, there is the picture of a charming stone house, seen above a hedge, and across a narrow lawn. The extreme left wall of the house merges subtly into a stone garden wall, coped with brick. Some bright flowers stand up before this wall, and before the house—but beyond these visible things, complete privacy and seclusion reign.

Approaching the house, a brick walk is seen to lead from the driveway across the whole lot to a gate at the far left end of the front garden wall. A turn of this walk leads directly to the front door, which admits to the smallest possible hallway, with rough plaster walls, and ceiling beams of hewn timber, stained brown. At the hall's end is a door giving upon the garden terrace—a place to be explored presently.

The main function of the hallway, aside from its stairs to the second floor, is to give access to the living-room, which, by virtue of a frank acceptance of the dimensional limitations of the whole house, is also the dining-room. The row of casements, in fact, which were at your left as you came in the front door, are the "dining-room" windows. In front of these windows, and along the wall at right angle, is a built-in bench, and paneling, and an ample and gracious refectory table is the dining-table. Step away from the table, and you are in the living-room, with its quiet, restful walls, dark woodwork, and a simple fireplace.

Upstairs there is presented an arrangement of the utmost compactness—three unbelievably comfortable bedrooms, two bathrooms, and plenty of closets. Two of the bedrooms, moreover, have fireplaces, and all have amply adequate (and very picturesque) windows. It seems as though everything that could reasonably be wanted is there, and that nothing there is superfluous. And, as may well be imagined, there is no waste space—with forty-six feet as the total length of the house, there was not any space available to waste.

Returning to the downstairs hall, you are about to go out into the garden, quite unaware that the ingenious plan of this extraordinary little house has not been entirely inspected. There must be a kitchen somewhere (certainly there could be no room for a maid), but you did not notice any evidence of a kitchen, either outside or inside.

Here is an illustration of the potency of the pictorial element in country house architecture. The whole profile of the little house, in its relation to the site, seemed so perfect and so charming that you did not notice the blank downstairs wall of the end of the T-shaped wing. A look at the plan will disclose not one, but two maids' rooms, an ample kitchen, refrigerator room, and back porch. And all this space was never missed, as you came into the house—the kitchen and maids' rooms were so skillfully disposed of that they might have been located in the furthermost wing of some great rambling manor house like Haddon Hall. More clever small house planning than this does not exist. It seems almost impossible that such complete isolation could be effected in so small a house.

With the plan at last explored, the garden is found to be beautifully consistent with the whole scheme. To adjust the pitch of the whole piece of ground toward its back-line, the house is set upon a pleasantly informal brick terrace, and is seen to possess, quite astonishingly, no "back"— it is as charmingly picturesque from the garden as it appeared from the road.

It is a walled garden, with its highest wall completely eliminating the garage, service court and back-door—the only communication being a quaint little postern gate, a door in an arched opening. There, in the garden, are flowers, and an informal flagged walk, all around about a central space of grass.

Along the left wall is a grape arbor, which continues on the terrace, covering the whole space formed by the end-wall of the house, and the wall that screens the garden from the road. Immediately beyond the back wall of the garden the ground falls away abruptly, so that only the upper branches of a dense grove of large trees appear above it—and in this corner is a brick-floored "belvedere"— a quaintly informal little summer house with a strangely and interestingly designed roof. When the sun is hot upon the terrace, it is cool in the belvedere, for an iron-grilled opening draws a breeze through it.

And, seated in the belvedere, you command a view of the entire domain—house and grounds, and realize the power of *design*, whereby on a small piece of ground, the owner has been given all, essentially, that could really be enjoyed or *used* if his estate covered a score of broad acres. The house and the garden can be lived in—there is not a brick or a stone wasted on mere vainglorious show. Every bit of the place is designed and made to be enjoyed and utilized—an architectural achievement of the highest order.

The illustrations show a house which makes "pictures" from any point of view. The plan has been explored, but another salient point is not to be overlooked. The materials are all honest, home-like things—local "Chestnut Hill" ledge stone, brick, and cement, with a shingle roof. Not only are the materials significant through their inherent qualities of texture and color, and also excellently appropriate to the character of the house, but they are used with a vigorous colloquialism that brings out their best qualities.

The execution, in other words, is as nice an architectural achievement as the ideas and plan-work that created the house.

At an earlier point something was said about harmony between architect and client. You would not imagine such a perfect little house emerging from discord, or the mutual recriminations which so often (and so unnecessarily) mar many an otherwise happy building project.

But this was not the case. Cause and result become confused in any conjecture as to whether the house is good because the relationship between architect and client was such a happy one, or whether the latter was so because the architect did the house so beautifully. It is very worthy of chronicle, however, that the relationship *was* a happy one, and that the clients were consistently in sympathy with the architect's sincere efforts to create a small house, on a small piece of ground, so conscientiously that it would attain, as nearly as possible, the ideal.

Such work as produced this house cannot be done unless it is inspired by absolute sincerity on the part of the architect. And the client's recognition of that sincerity should take the form it took in this instance—the form of confidence.

Generally speaking, far too little confidence is reposed in architects, and in others who are earnestly trying to do creative work.

The house which forms the subject of this article stands forth as an example of the eminently satisfactory results that come from a certain kind of faith—faith in the architect, and abstention from coercing him and overruling him at every turn. Houses very seldom turn out unsuccessfully under the hands of an able architect, but numberless houses have turned out unsuccessfully because of a client's insistence on some fundamentally unwise changes. Let us give our architects and designers every chance to do their best and most inspired work. They have everything to gain and nothing to lose by doing their best.

In this admirable little house there is a sociological as well as an architectural aspect to consider. It is, in many ways, a symbol of a new era, of a whole set of new standards, and very excellent ones. It typifies a new and really sincere kind of simplicity quite different from the "cult" of simplicity that duped many of our least simple people a few years ago. It typifies a kind of simplicity that is a fact, not a fad. Nothing about this house, or about its grounds, is in any way pretentious. Materials, design, planning and furniture all reflect a new sincerity, a new freedom from affectation. There is apparent neither the affectation that seeks to convey an impression of grandeur, nor the affectation that seeks to convey an impression of "the simple life," consciously "staged."

There are a great many new valuations in effect since the war. A great many people are wanting simple, straightforward things, free from much of the unusable excess which was once indulged in for show. At one time houses were built more for the edification of the passerby than for the use, comfort or domestic economy of the people who were to live in them. Why, otherwise, was it considered so desirable, even essential as an index of social standing, to have a perfectly useless and artistically distressing "cupola" on every mansard-roofed "mansion?"

It is very doubtful if people will ever do that particular kind of foolish thing again. Our sense of values, and perhaps our sense of humor, has improved. So many things have worked against sincere architectural expression in this country—and one of the worst, from 1830 or thereabouts, until well past 1896, was self-consciousness—from which we are not yet entirely free.

Colonial architecture, and early American architecture—especially the former—were straightforward and simple expressions of actual needs, in terms dictated by actual conditions. They did not try to build better houses than they could afford, and, most important of all, they did not build for show.

Even the larger houses of today are beginning to assume a new kind of good taste, a new architectural and social integrity. There is less pretense and far more straightforward expression of honest needs and preferences. Country houses in general are taking on more of the aspect of dwellings.

But architects cannot bring this about unaided. The tastes and ideals of their clients must ever play a powerful part in the development of architecturally fine and honest country houses. The mental attitude of the client toward life in general, and toward the kind of life which he, in particular, intends to live, must ultimately exert more influence upon domestic architecture than the heritage of all European architecture, and the successive fashions which are called styles, and which clothe but fail to inspire the work of the architect.

It is because of these things that I think this little Philadelphia country house, which gives its owners all that they really require, actually is a symbol not only of the highest order of architectural achievement for its type, but a symbol as well of a new and better America.

MATLACK PRICE.

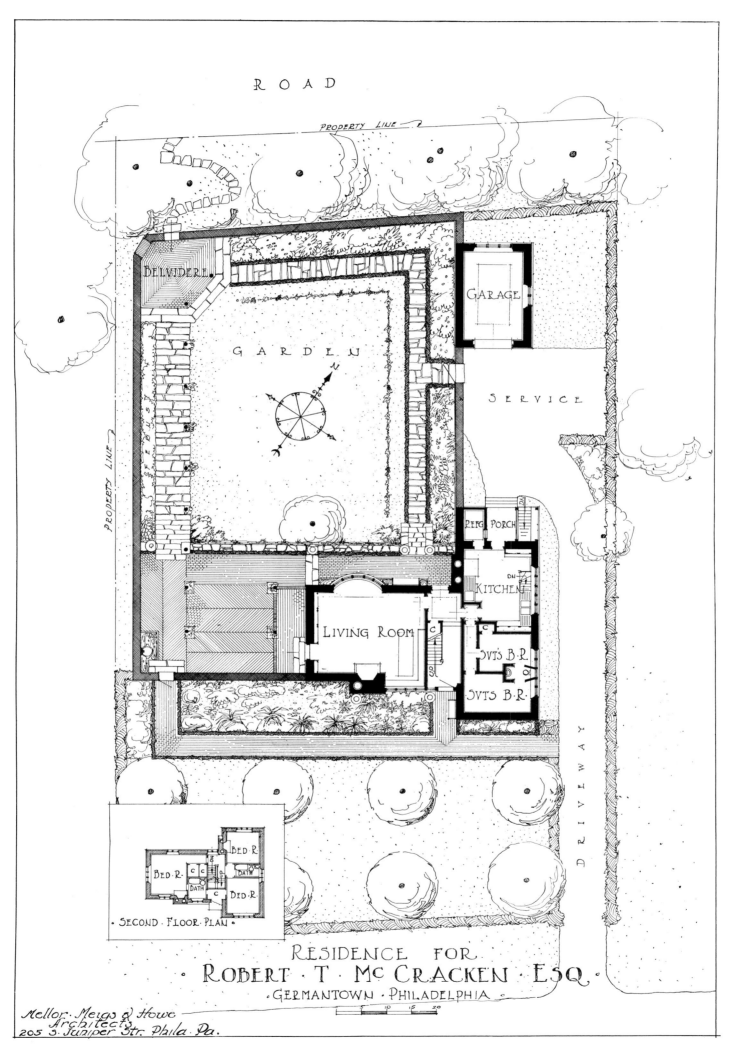

ROAD

PROPERTY LINE

BELVIDERE.

GARAGE

GARDEN

SERVICE

N

REF'G PORCH

KITCHEN

PROPERTY LINE

LIVING ROOM

SVTS B·R·

SVTS B·R·

DRIVEWAY

BED·R·

BED·R·

BATH

BATH

BED·R·

SECOND·FLOOR·PLAN·

RESIDENCE FOR
· ROBERT · T · Mc CRACKEN · ESQ ·
· GERMANTOWN · PHILADELPHIA ·

5   10   15   20

Mellor· Meigs & Howe
Architects
205 S Juniper Str. Phila Pa.

PLAN

ENTRANCE SIDE

HIGH WALL BETWEEN HOUSE AND GARAGE

WIDE BED ON ENTRANCE SIDE

FRONT DOOR ANGLE

SECOND STORY HALLWAY

BOOK CASES IN LIVING ROOM

FOUNTAIN IN GRAPE ROOM

DINING END OF LIVING ROOM

SIDEBOARD AND SERVING TABLE IN LIVING ROOM

HOUSE FROM THE BOTTOM OF THE GARDEN

GARDEN TERRACE

THE BELVEDERE

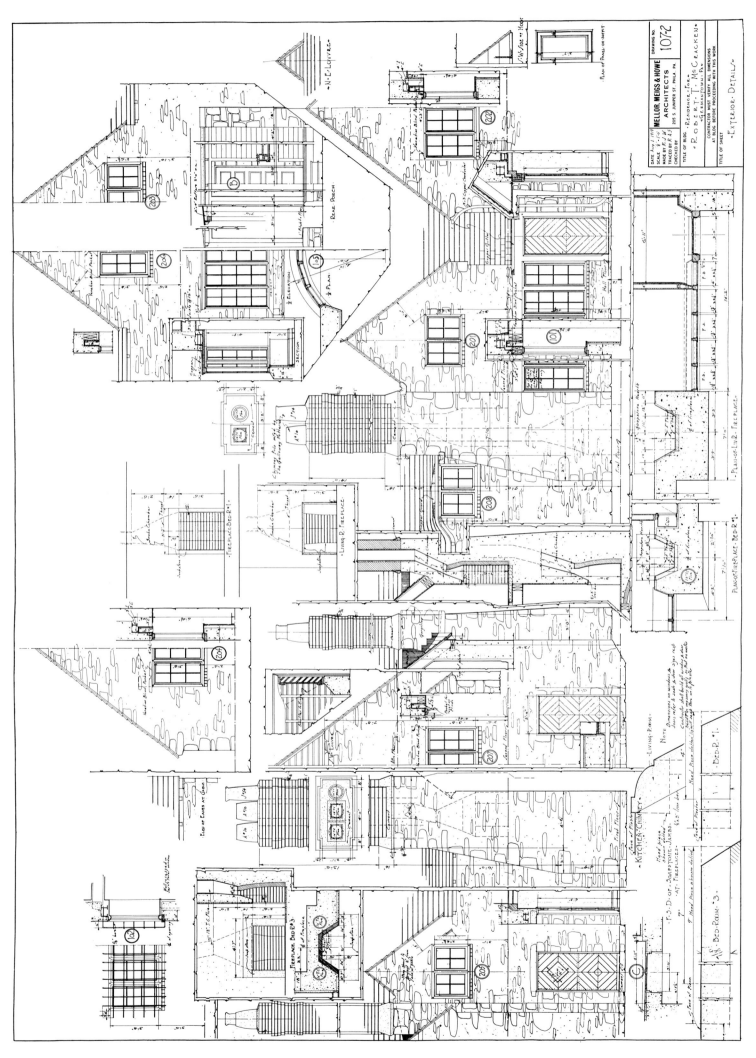

EXTERIOR DETAILS

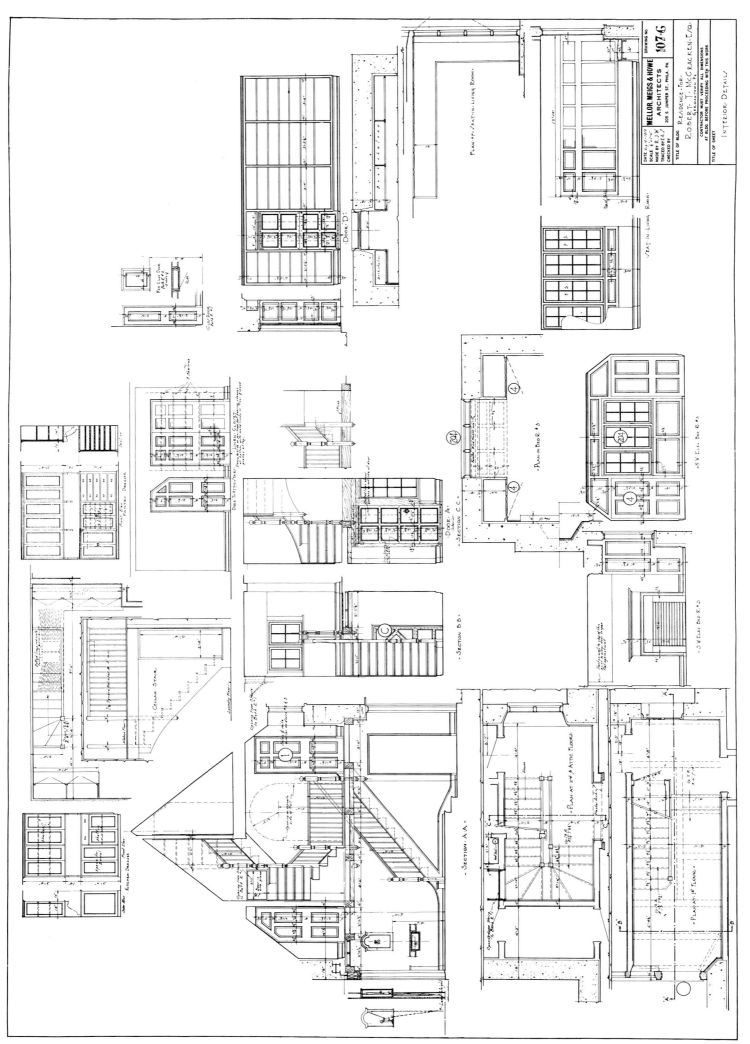

INTERIOR DETAILS

THE RESIDENCE OF HEATLY C. DULLES, ESQ.
VILLA NOVA, PA.

REPRINTED FROM THE JANUARY, 1921, ISSUE OF "THE ARCHITECTURAL RECORD"

A VERY low, sinuous and flowing outline enclosing a mass, sombre though warm in color, is my first impression of this house. From the lower road it stands upon a firm, long line of wall so generous, simple and sturdy in its purpose of retaining the scheme that were there little else of accomplishment the house would have that comfortable stability so much to be desired and so seldom had.

How often we see dry and loosely laid walls retaining terraces and garden arrangements immediately adjacent to the house—surely a very crumbling and unconvincing substructure to encounter at the base of a solid house mass. It is good to observe that the architects, alive to this pitfall, have not only felt the wisdom of establishing a simple, solid surface of wall to carry their scheme and give telling value to the details of the building, but that they have strengthened the impression of stability with the appropriate use of buttresses. Beyond are the screen walls of the garden and connecting link 'twixt house and garage, sheltering all from the north and adding firmness and final conviction to a total scheme of good sense and real beauty.

It is not for us to say this style or manner of building is appropriate and that one is not. Nor is it for us to exclude from consideration manifestations in the field of art that fall without the limited realm which is closest to the heart and which we think to be our own. But it is for us to be quick to see the fruits of minds working with sincerity and enthusiasm, and I confess that I do not find a line in this building which does not possess these qualities in generous measure, refreshing indeed in days of mingled pedantry and doubtful originality.

The exterior is a direct reflection of the interior, and at no point is there any evidence of forcing the one to suit the other. In fact, what intimacy and charm has gathered round the garden front is simply an indication of what is taking place inside.

I have often thought how meaningless, in their effort to be quaint, are the exteriors of many of our houses. I think it is because one forgets that the chief excuse for a house is to shelter the life within it. So soon as we conceive our design from the outside in, or view outside and inside as separate problems, then does architecture become the shallow thing it too often is. An architect of some eminence once told me that it was quite possible to clothe a given plan in any "style." Judging from the examples of his work, this has evidently been his guiding principle; but with what success I forbear to say. Beauty is not a quality that can be applied "on the side."

We hear it said without qualification that what our architecture lacks is color. Surely this is true enough if we observe that for the most part we seem able to do little better than waver between stupid and broadcast use of grey and the garish juxtaposition of broken colors. In this house, however, we have color and surface quality playing a most important and satisfactory rôle. The rough stone walls have been pointed or almost completely hidden by a material evidently composed of cement, lime and a light neutral brown gravel. The surface is not forbiddingly rough and affected, nor is it without feeling and hard. It has been produced by using a rather crude tool in skilled and thoughtful hands. The inconspicuous metal casement windows and their plain oak frames, left without finish to gather the patine of time, are modest and beautifully subordinated to the wall surfaces.

The site offered little in natural advantages. With the exception of woods to the east and a very pleasant meadow and distant prospect to the south, the architects have had little within or without the bounds of the property to assist them, and much in the way of suburban mediocrity around them and rubbing shoulders with their scheme. A rather fortuitous absence of seclusion will be overcome when the plan for the development of the property is carried out. Here, indeed, is a delightful opportunity for both architects and owner. With the most provident existence of finished levels and walls, there remains that most illusive and sensitive task of gardening and planting. If this be accomplished in the spirit and manner which has inspired the building, I shall have had restored my faith in the American mind to conceive, beyond a few admitted exceptions, anything of note in landscape architecture. How much of inspiration we are able to draw from the continent in our buildings, and how little in that endless field of activities beyond their walls.

Within, as without the house, there is evidence of the same eagerness for interest in a balanced informality of composition. As the plan will show, all the rooms are nicely distributed along the southern side of a narrow hall, whose axis is fortunately terminated in a wall niche across the garden. Each room is discovered in pleasant sequence and according to the privacy it should enjoy. This rather loose arrangement of plan is no simple task, and it is rarely indeed that we see it accomplished with such reason and evident meaning. The bookroom is properly found in the most private quarter of the house, giving on to a diminutive and secluded garden.

To me the dining room is quite the *chef d'oeuvre* and, barring a slight tendency toward too much movement in the plaster ceiling pattern, is most satisfying. It is unfortunate that a photograph cannot be had that will give adequately the impression of this room. The view here given, looking into the corner of the dining room, showing the steps rising to the living room, is a beautifully imaginative composition in iron, oak and stone, and is only one of three such delightful little vestibules that persistently punctuate the plan and reoccur in most musical fashion.

The rooms within this charming country house would stand by themselves; they are interesting and lovely in proportion, arrangement and detail, and to the grounds without has been given that simple development of line and mass and form that alone can impart the feeling of completeness to a scheme; ample proof, indeed, that a skilled and dominant professional force has been working in conjunction with a very sympathetic and gracious client.

EDMUND B. GILCHRIST.

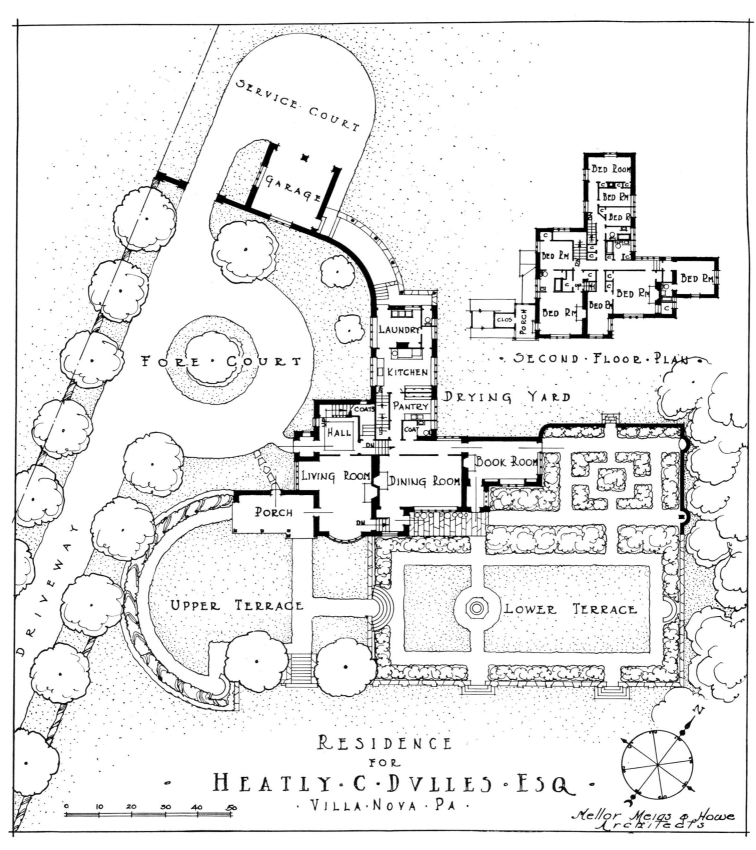

SERVICE · COURT

GARAGE

BED ROOM
BED RM
BED R
BED RM
BED RM
BED RM
BED RM
BED RM
CLOS
PORCH

· SECOND · FLOOR · PLAN ·

FORE · COURT

LAUNDRY

KITCHEN

DRYING YARD

COATS
PANTRY
COAT

HALL
DN

BOOK ROOM

LIVING ROOM
DINING ROOM

DRIVEWAY

PORCH
DN

UPPER TERRACE

LOWER TERRACE

N

RESIDENCE
FOR
· HEATLY · C · DVLLES · ESQ ·
· VILLA · NOVA · PA ·

0   10   20   30   40   50

Mellor Meigs & Howe
Architects

PLAN

FROM ENTRANCE DRIVE

FROM FORECOURT   DOOR TO DINING ROOM VESTIBULE

FROM SERVICE GATE

HEATLY C. DULLES, ESQ., VILLA NOVA, PA.

1917

PORCH

ENTRANCE

79

SOUTHWEST WINDOW OF LIVING ROOM

HALL

LIVING ROOM FIREPLACE

HEATLY C. DULLES, ESQ., VILLA NOVA, PA.

1917

DINING ROOM VESTIBULE

FIRST FLOOR HALL

SECOND FLOOR HALL

BOOK ROOM FROM WITHIN

BOOK ROOM FROM WITHOUT

HEATLY C. DULLES, ESQ., VILLA NOVA, PA.

1917

SOUTHEAST FRONT

UPPER AND LOWER TERRACES

LIVING ROOM BAY

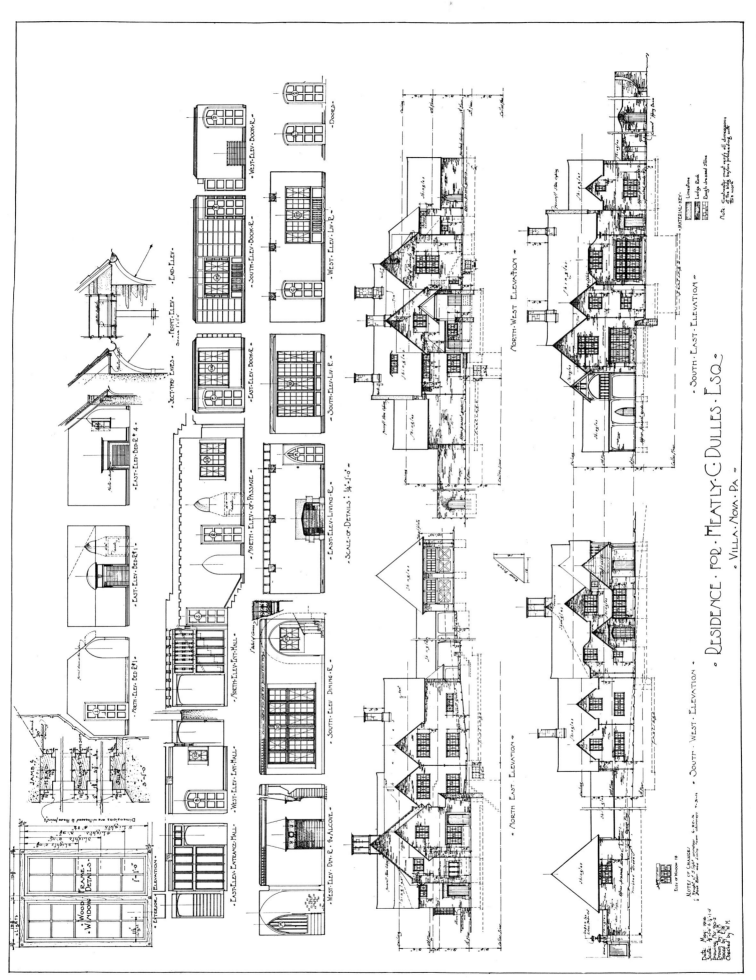

ELEVATIONS AND SECTIONS

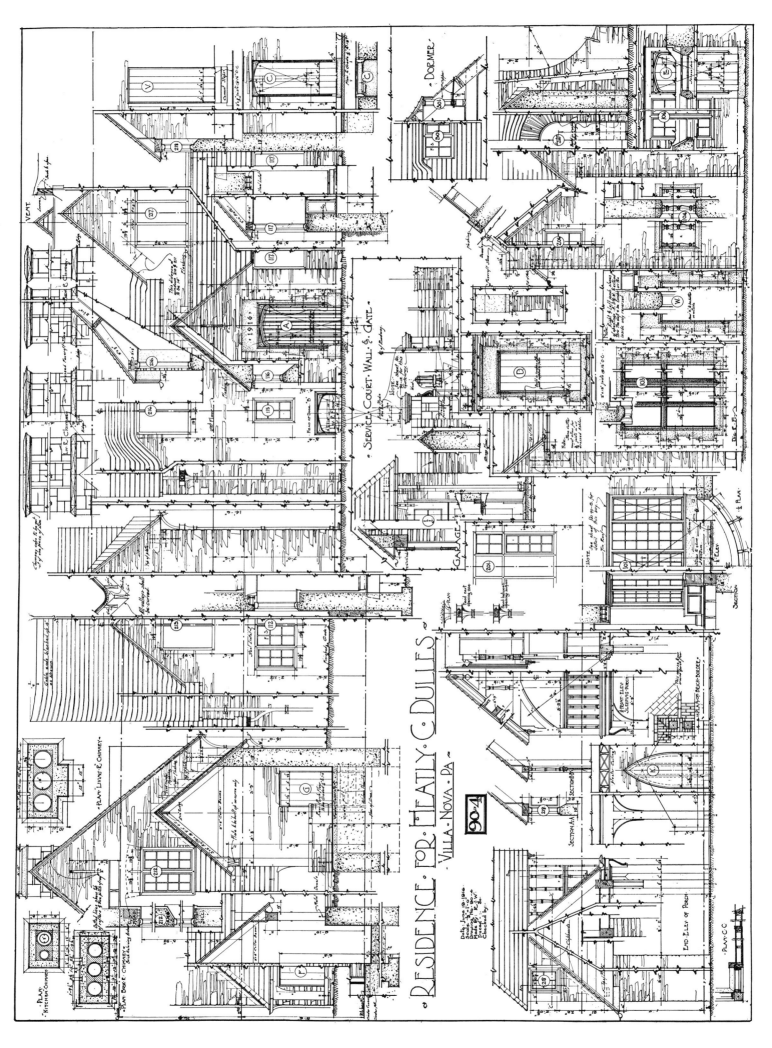

EXTERIOR DETAILS

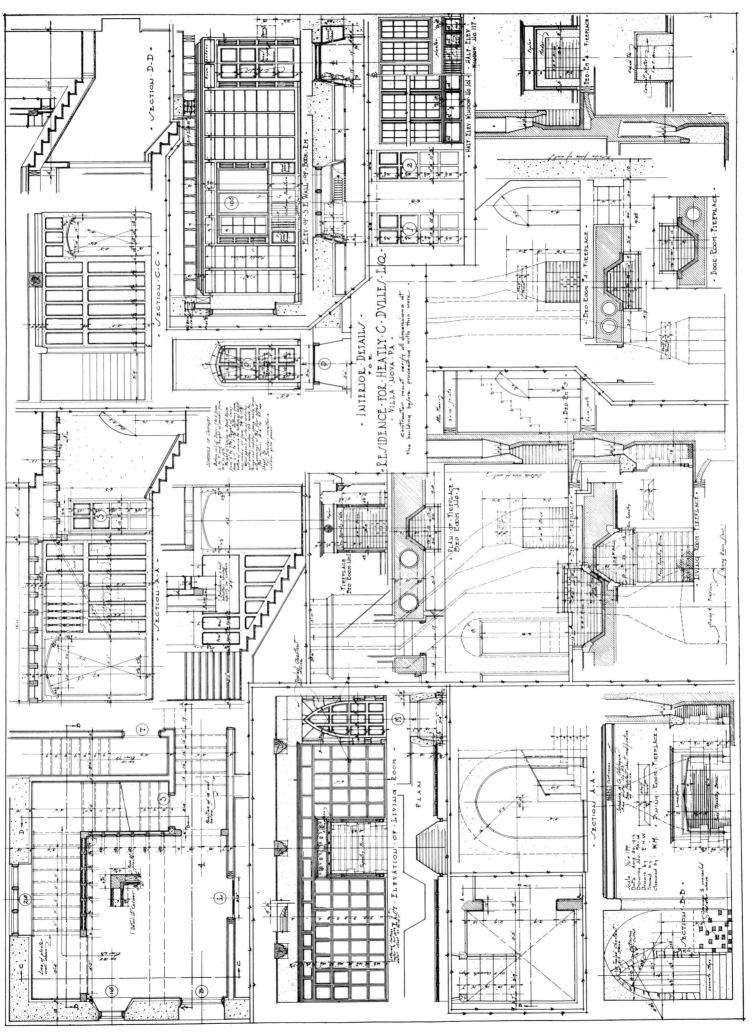

INTERIOR DETAILS

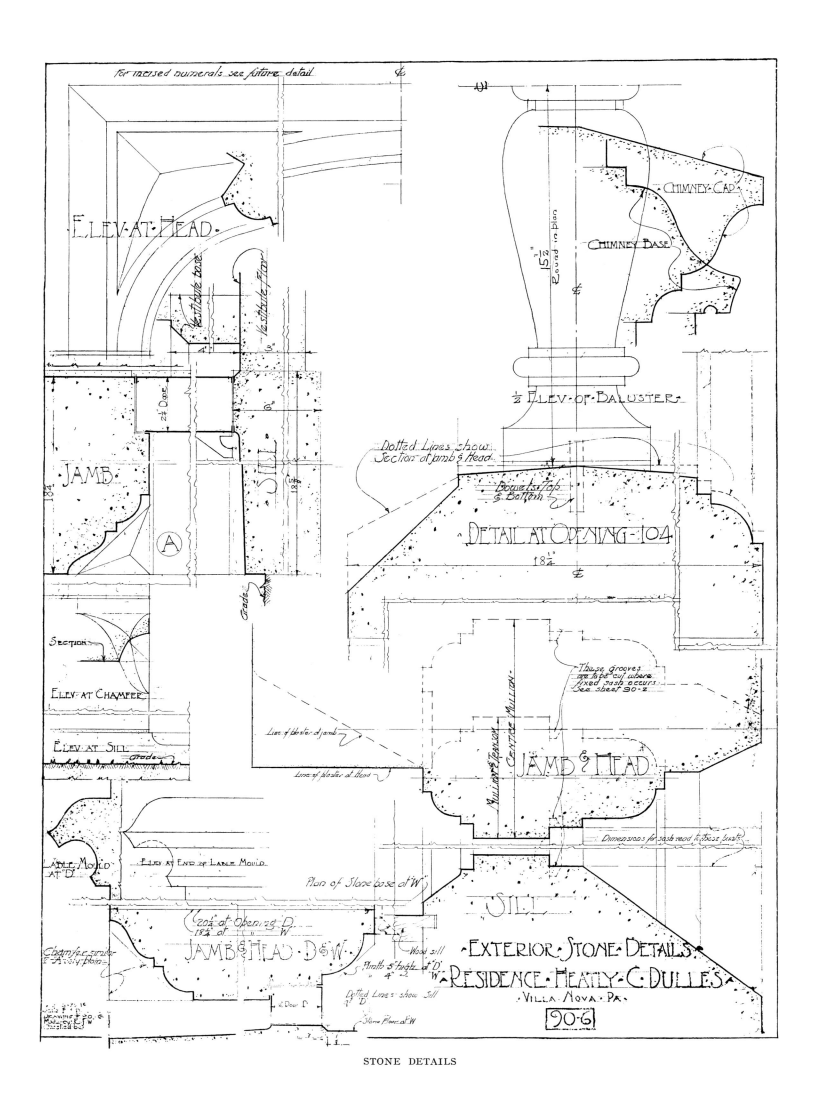

STONE DETAILS

THE HOUSE OF LEONARD T. BEALE, ESQ.
ST. DAVIDS, PENNA.

A S THE floor plans accompanying the photographs of Mr. Beale's place show only the arrangement inside the house, it may be well to give a brief description of some of the more important outside surroundings.

This property, located in what is called a "development," contains only one-third of an acre and is closely surrounded by other houses. Its orientation is perfect, looking out to the southeast over the St. Davids Golf Course with the entrance side to the northwest, facing the railroad, which is quite near. The property is wedge-shaped, with the two side lines diverging towards the Golf Course, thus making it possible to allow this pleasant outlook to play the principal role in the whole design.

Since the "parti" of a "long and low" house was assumed, the design was made to extend from one side of the lot to the other, the Garage being used as a screen to the Service Yard from the entrance side, while an ivy-clad wall, (shown on page 90, but not on the plans) separates the services from the living part of the scheme. On the other side, there is another wall, with Lombardy poplar trees behind it, which forms the barrier to the adjoining property on the southwest.

A T-shaped plan was used and, than this, it is difficult to discover anything more practical or economical—once having assumed a plan from which was to grow a "one-room-thick" house. With the hall and stairs situated at the junction of the two bars of the T, distribution to all rooms is extremely easy and convenient, and the "one-room-thick" characteristic, like anything else in architecture, has advantages and disadvantages of its own. It makes more outside walls, both to build, and to keep warm in winter, than a square plan; but it also brings better opportunity for distribution of windows and for cross ventilation, while the exterior that springs from such a plan seems to be restful, and comfortable almost of its own accord. In this instance it was possible to locate all the important rooms overlooking the Golf Course and away from the railroad.

Rigid economy in ornament and detail was the watchword throughout, and it is interesting to note that all the trees, hedges, vines, etc., which play such an important part in the place as it exists today, were planted as a part of the original scheme, and at a cost of less than $150.00.

A certain apprehension was felt in the beginning as to the salability of a house as unusual in character as this one was at the time it was built,—namely, the early part of 1912; but it has already changed hands twice, both times at an increasing figure, and was sold in 1922 for more than twice its original cost.

ENTRANCE SIDE

SIDE TOWARDS GOLF COURSE

ENTRANCE ANGLE

SERVICE GABLES

LIVING ROOM BAY AND FIREPLACE

LEONARD T. BEALE, ESQ., ST. DAVIDS, PA.

1912

GOLF COURSE THROUGH LIVING ROOM BAY

WISTARIA TRELLIS

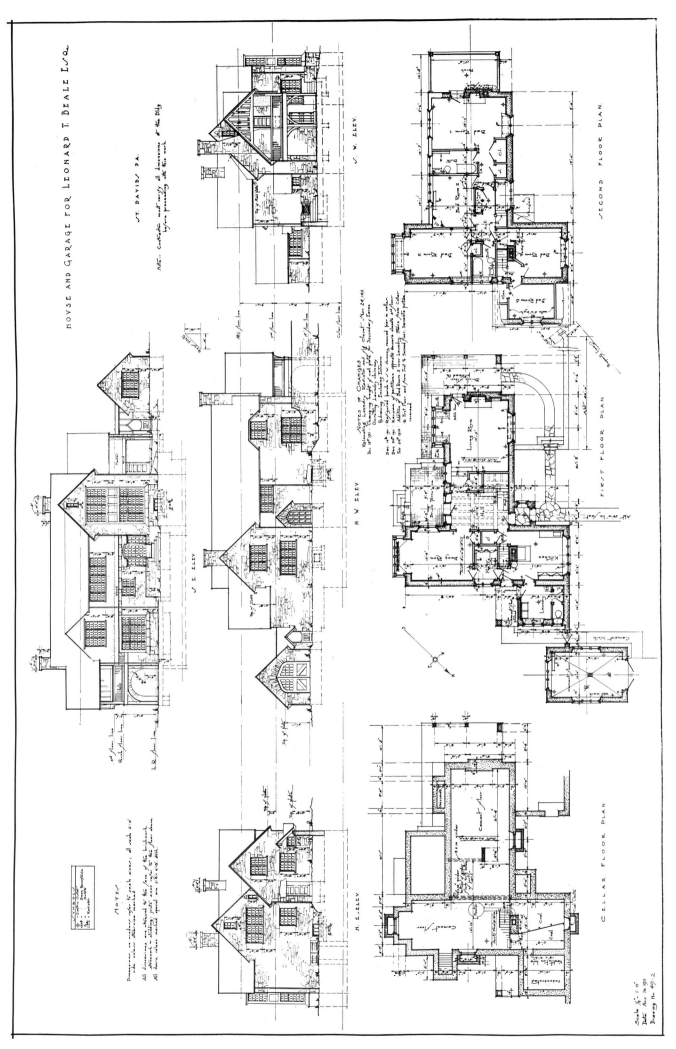

PLANS AND ELEVATIONS

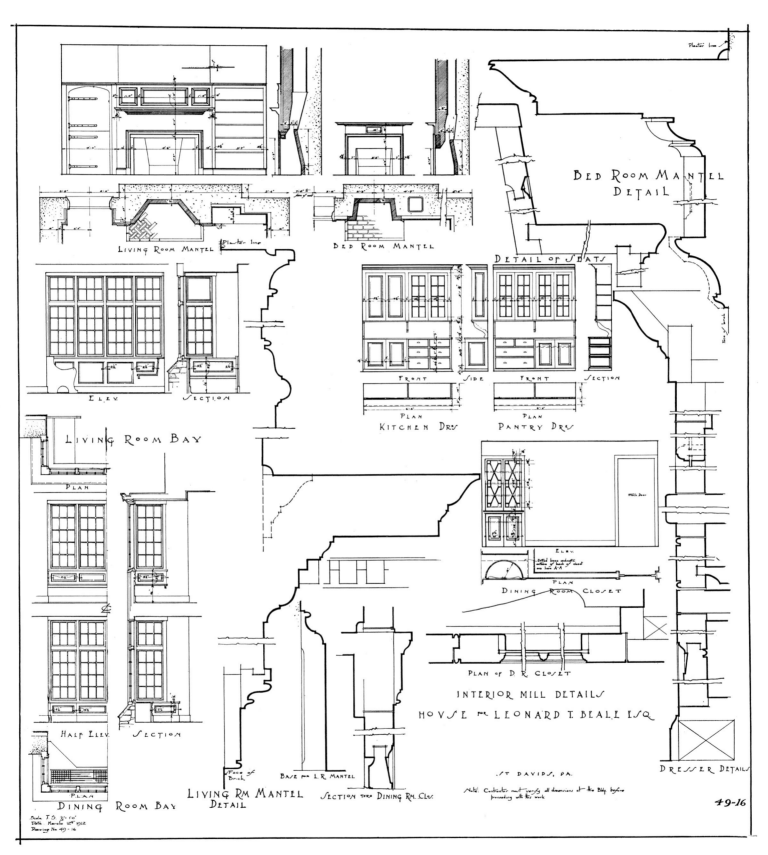

INTERIOR DETAILS

THE DEVELOPMENT OF THE COUNTRY RESIDENCE OF
MRS. ARTHUR V. MEIGS, RADNOR, PA.

REPRINTED FROM THE MARCH, 1922, ISSUE OF COUNTRY LIFE

THERE is, perhaps, no better way of beginning an article such as the present one than by saying a few words on the subject of permanence.

The property under consideration, at Radnor, Pa., was acquired by the owner sixteen years ago. The original house was built some three or four years prior to its purchase, and at that time it is fair to say that there was practically nothing on the place save the house and stable. It is suggested to the reader that, if he or she be interested at all, more than a passing glance be given to the plan which appears on page 100, for in the plan lies the meat of the whole matter. Though the lettering is inevitably small, owing to limitations of space, the titles which designate the various elements that comprise the whole tell their own story and carry their own inference. "Pastures" imply cows, "Chicken Yards" imply chickens, "Paddocks" imply horses, "Vegetables" imply something good to eat in summer, "Poikiles," "Sunset Towers," "Potagers," "Dipping Tanks," "Paduan Gardens," and so forth, all imply another state of mind, and the sum total implies a world of what a great many people have definitely settled in their minds to be an unutterable amount of trouble. And yet it must be remembered that this is a comparatively small and simple place, as the cuts clearly show, and includes in its entirety but twenty-three acres.

If one does not want to be bothered with cows and chickens and vegetable patches and strawberry beds and lilacs and Paduan gardens and the rest of it—for there is no possible question that they entail unending care and attention and infinite vexation—one had much better not live in the country at all. One had better rent a nice suite of apartments in a thickly settled district, conveniently located, and have two or three high powered limousines from which to view the country at ease should the fancy strike one. One will then be altogether free of the pains and anxieties of a country life — free of the pains, and free of the joys, as well. It will cost just about the same.

It is obvious at a glance that such a plan as the one under consideration could not possibly have been conceived and executed all at one time. If an architect had produced such a medley by a single effort we should be entirely justified in supposing him to be mad. It is obviously an organic growth, and an organic growth requires time in which to develop. An architect did not produce it. It grew—like "Topsy." And how can a place grow outside of the idea of permanence? If one rents a piece of land, or if one builds a house with the idea of how salable the house will be, and how much profit one can make on one's money over and above what one has put into it, uppermost in one's mind, one starts with a point of view inimical to a successful result. If one lives only for business and if the pleasures of life are forced into the hard framework of the business point of view, this animating spirit will, of a certainty, appear in everything that one does. The object in having a place is to live in it; not to sell it. If the spirit of barter is to play a prominent part, if purchase and sale enter into it, why not operate in the stock market, where everything is arranged for that particular purpose and the whole matter is a clean-cut business proposition. A country place should be, and generally is, quite the antithesis of a clean-cut business proposition.

The whole discussion terminates, as most discussions do, in the question of a state of mind. If the state of mind is right, it doesn't much matter what you do, it all comes right in the end. We can make a thousand mistakes in detail, but if our fundamental basic idea is adhered to, and if that fundamental idea is fortunate enough to have been right in the first place, the mass of what follows from the hypothesis cannot fail to reflect the state of mind in which we began.

How does one have anything nice? By loving it. And can one have anything nice without loving it? No. And can one love a transient thing? We think not. It is scarcely worth while to begin; so we come back to our original idea of permanence, and find it quite fundamental. We might have a permanent thing which was nice, and we might have a permanent thing which was not, but we could not have a nice thing which was not permanent. As well to suppose that a transient weed holds the same place in the scheme of things as the oak, or as the oak in turn holds to light. The highest aspirations of mankind turn ever toward permanence, and never reach it. It is an ideal to be sought, not a thing capable of attainment.

However, no matter how far one may fall short of reaching what one is aiming at, it is better to aim at something than at nothing, and whether the process be conscious or unconscious does not concern us. This place at Radnor is the result of practically sixteen years of continual care and interest.

The property lies along the ridge of a hill, and it may be roughly said that the main road from the east entrance to the west entrance runs along this ridge, with the land falling away both to the north and to the south, and giving an impression, as the photographs show, of a place almost wooded, certainly thickly covered with trees throughout—perhaps in almost too great profusion, for any property owner soon realizes that it is more difficult to cut down a tree than to plant it.

One of the first steps in development was the starting of the nursery, which is shown in the view from the sunset tower (page 103) at the end of the vista. This nursery was started at an initial cost of $10, that being the price of 1,000 trees at a penny each, and it is interesting to note that the trees by the sunset tower (page 104) which, at the time the photograph was taken, were only half out in the spring, came from this same nursery and have grown to the size that they now are from seedlings no bigger than the lead in a pencil. This vista from the sunset tower was quite accidental. It started as a grass walk in the vegetable patch and served the humble purpose of furnishing communication from one end to the other—in short, an obvious service path. It seemed that a little room could be spared from the space for the vegetables, and a few flowers happened to creep in; the sunset tower, entirely for reasons of its own and to be dealt with later, happened to get built right on this particular corner of the potager, and it seemed lucky that the path happened to be there; the nursery was in the way, so the nursery had a hole drilled through it, and presto! a full-fledged architectural trick, arrived at in a most undignified and non-architectural manner!

Owing to the absence of trees and therefore of shade on the place, one of the first adjuncts to the house that was built was the so-called "poikile," shown in relation to the house on pages 101 and 102, while the doorway, on page 103, is in the centre of the central wall. This building is nothing more than an outside porch. The idea was derived from Hadrian's Villa, near Rome, where the poikile was hundreds of yards long, but this simple affair consists merely of a central wall, pierced by a door, and surrounded by columns, as is shown in the cuts. Its advantages are somewhat obvious in that being built free from the house it darkens none of the rooms, while with its central wall running east and west it affords either sunshine or shade, as is desired, and according to the weather. The central doorway looking through to the Paduan garden and fountain gives the added advantage of being built to afford shade and air simultaneously if so desired.

An analysis of the design of the poikile may not be out of place in this connection.

One of the most malignant diseases to which designers are subject is the transplanting of architectural elements from their original surroundings to new and far different ones without the realization that he who does the transplanting will, or should be, held to strict accountability for any results which may ensue. If one changes a preposition or a pronoun in a line of poetry, if one shifts a comma or changes it to a semicolon, if one adapts a quotation from the Bible to one's own purposes and makes a plural out of a singular to meet the special needs of the case, let it be remembered that the new line of poetry or the new quotation has become the property of its new owner and not that of the original author, and let this new owner keep firmly fixed in his mind the question of strict accountability and perhaps he will then be inclined to proceed with greater caution, provided, of course, that he is a reverend fellow to begin with. To translate Shakespeare into another language, the translator must have an equally good understanding of both languages and, in addition, his command of the other language must be equal to Shakespeare's command of English, his mind must be as great, his soul must be as great, and he must be the equal of Shakespeare as a poet. Such an one is rare among translators.

Is it not the soundest way to look at it that the creator of the copied thing shall act as its sole sponsor, and that the adaptation shall rest solely upon its own merits?

Into this category of adapted motives the poikile immediately falls and must stand for judgment. A building which consists of a free standing wall surrounded by wood columns eight feet high and set about eight feet on centres with pediments at either end looks just about enough like a Greek temple to make us think "what a falling off is there." But at this point another factor is introduced, for the thing is so extremely useful and so extremely practical that as the trees grow up around it, and the Paduan garden grows up in front of it, and the flower pots get set out around the edge of it, some of its obvious architectural defects become mercifully lost sight of, and the comforting saying comes into our mind that "Ivy is to the architect as sod is to the physician."

It will, perhaps, at this point, be well to explain some of the titles which appear upon the plan, and with all due apologies to those who already know, a dipping tank is a small cistern filled with water, such as the one shown on page 101. The method of supplying the water and the form of the design may vary as desired, but the principal feature is that the surface of the water shall be about two feet from the ground so that a person about to draw a vessel of water is freed of the necessity of waiting while the water runs and may get it at once by dipping the vessel into the tank. A ha-ha wall is a wall (generally from three to four feet high) built against a cut in a bank, and constitutes a barrier or fence for cattle, anything being able to fall down from the top, but the cattle being unable to get up from the bottom. Its advantage is that it keeps the cattle in the pasture while no barrier is visible from the upper side; by its use in this case the lawn and north pasture appear as one when seen from the house. The name of the sunset tower explains itself, and a description of the poikile has already been given. A potager is a vegetable garden brightened with flowers. The word *potager* is French and the thing itself is almost universal in France. It begins as a thing of utility and ends as a thing of beauty, and perhaps, after all, nothing could be more satisfactory than that. No hard and fast rules govern its design or size, but the one shown on the plan is typical of thousands in Europe. The vegetables are in the big spaces and the flowers and dwarf fruit trees lie along the walks.

The sunset tower is the result of a desire for more light and the conviction that a vegetable patch is about as pleasant a thing to look at as anything that may be found. As the trees from the ten-dollar nursery were moved to their permanent or semi-permanent locations, and their growth went on year by year, the poikile, which had at first served as the centre of life outdoors, began to acquire a shut-in feeling; and the wish for a more comprehensive view of the whole property, and to be able once more to see the sunset, led to the building of this tower on the northwest corner of the potager. As the bridge is to a ship, so is this tower to this country place. It commands a view to the north, south, east, and west. Here one may sit to watch the sunset, and after that the stars. When the sun, the traditional enemy of our almost tropical summers, has left his burning firmament, it affords an opportunity to forsake the trees, our allies throughout the day, and gratify the human instinct on a summer night to approach a little nearer to the sky.

The chauffeur's, farmer's, and butler's cottages, and the barn on the other side of the Old Lancaster Road, were all acquired a year or so after the purchase of the original property, and together with the wood yard, manure and compost yard, tool house, coldframes, etc., located beside the orchard, play a very important part in the administration of the place.

But the most important room in the house is the so-called "garden room," shown on page 102, which is located between the house and the poikile, and was built in 1920. The poikile, built in 1906, was kept at a sufficient distance from the house to permit of the building of this room as a future possibility, which did not materialize, however, for fourteen years. Perhaps it may be fairly said that the room was designed from the inside out rather than from the outside in. If the house is anything it is Colonial, and whatever may be the faults of the garden room no one could accuse it of being Colonial. It has metal casement windows in two groups of four and five lights, it has a chimney that looks more like a Tudor than like any Colonist, it is thoroughly unbalanced: the chimney is on the corner, the fireplace isn't in the middle, there is a niche holding a mid-Victorian statue on the outside, and next to that a door on an angle set under a coved corner with a fly screen that isn't standard, and a door that has a round head and Italian ironwork on the outside, with a square head on the inside, Colonial detail, and a French lock! The furniture ranges further, covering Chinese, a rough oak refectory table, a dainty Adam desk, and a large, thoroughly comfortable, somewhat ugly, and extremely expensive davenport of the most modern and up-to-date variety. Such a galaxy may somewhat alarm the more timid reader, but if he or she will look closely at the photograph of this room it will be seen that design is not altogether absent. The large davenport is placed in a position not altogether unfavorable. One may lie on one's back and look out the door with nothing in the way to prevent one from seeing through the spider-web fly screen all the way to a horizon half a mile away with a lone Lombardy poplar closing the vista. If it is winter, and some one will be kind enough to shut the door and light the fire, the same indolent occupant of the davenport, by a slight movement of his or her head, may regard the fire with equal ease. Should he or she desire to read, no necessity exists for getting up and dragging a chair to a position where there is light; the light is already there, exactly in the place that it is wanted. On the right of the chimneypiece there is a closet, and the closet contains wood and kindling and newspapers; the panel to the left of the fireplace is solid because the space back of it is occupied by the lady in the niche who stands outside; and to the left of that again the next two panels are doors, one on the straight and one on the angle, and these two doors open and reveal a flower sink which gives the room its name of "garden room." These two doors are fastened shut by an ornamental iron latch not picked out of a hardware catalogue, but specially designed to fit the special conditions brought about by two doors coming together in an altogether unconventional and non-standard style. We are persuaded that such considerations are as well entitled to a place in architecture as matters of style, period furniture, silhouettes of moldings, use of materials, the balance of elements, and all the rest of the patter with which we are almost done to death.

Special mention must be made of the spider-web fly screen. It is perhaps safe to say that no opening covered with a fly screen is as pleasant as one that is not, and therefore the problem of designing a fly screen resolves itself into an effort to mitigate an evil rather than to eliminate it. It may be said that fly screens are a necessity. But porches are a necessity; sleeping porches are a necessity; heating systems, radiators, electric lights, garages, all are necessities, and the essence of artistic development lies in making virtues out of necessities. The ancients carried the principle to a point where every household utensil, every plate, spoon, basin—in fact all the articles in every day use, among the poor as well as among the rich—became a thing of beauty as well as of utility.

If a fly screen is a necessity it should bear some relation to the surroundings in which it is to go, not be put on as an afterthought. The complexity of our problem has been very much increased over the problem faced by the ancients because our lives have become so infinitely more complex.

This fly screen attempts to be a thing of beauty and to mitigate the disadvantages of its own existence. As an inspiration for a fly screen, a spider web seems logical, the original being designed to catch flies for the spider to eat, and the iron and copper one under consideration being designed to catch flies and thus prevent them from eating those who live in the room. Nothing else would have fitted the opening so well, for fly screens with round headed tops and curved sections (page 103) cannot be had from stock, and perhaps the explanation is that the opening and the fly screen were not designed separately and by different minds, but were all born together.

In conclusion, it is with hesitation that the attempt has been made to write about anything from so close a relationship as the property under discussion must, of necessity, bear to the author of this article. The closer we stand to anything the more difficult it is to see it in its true proportions. The faults of the place are legion, but if any merit exists, we are persuaded that it is the result of the state of mind, a description of which was attempted at the beginning of this article. At the risk of becoming tiresome, the various elements which are perfectly clearly presented by the plan have been recapitulated in the text in the hope that the presentation of the subject might thus be somewhat clarified, but the plan itself, without photographs or article, tells the whole story.

ARTHUR I. MEIGS.

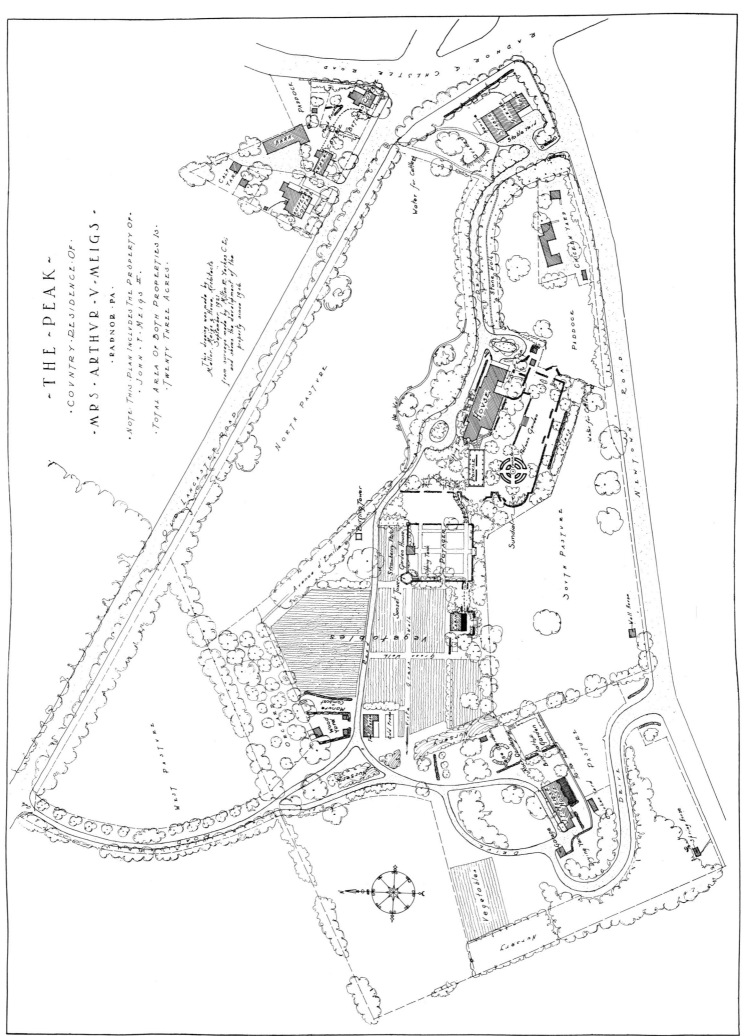

PLAN

GARDEN ROOM FROM POIKILE

WEST END OF GARDEN ROOM AND POIKILE

ESTATE OF MRS. ARTHUR V. MEIGS, RADNOR, PA.

1921

ANGLE BETWEEN GARDEN ROOM AND HOUSE

FIREPLACE WALL OF GARDEN ROOM

DOORWAY IN CENTRAL WALL OF POIKILE

SPIDER-WEB FLY-SCREEN FROM WITHOUT

VEGETABLE GARDEN FROM SUNSET TOWER

GRILLE ON SUNSET TOWER

ESTATE OF MRS. ARTHUR V. MEIGS, RADNOR, PA.

1921

SUNSET TOWER FROM OUTSIDE OF POTAGER

SPIDER-WEB FLY-SCREEN FROM WITHIN

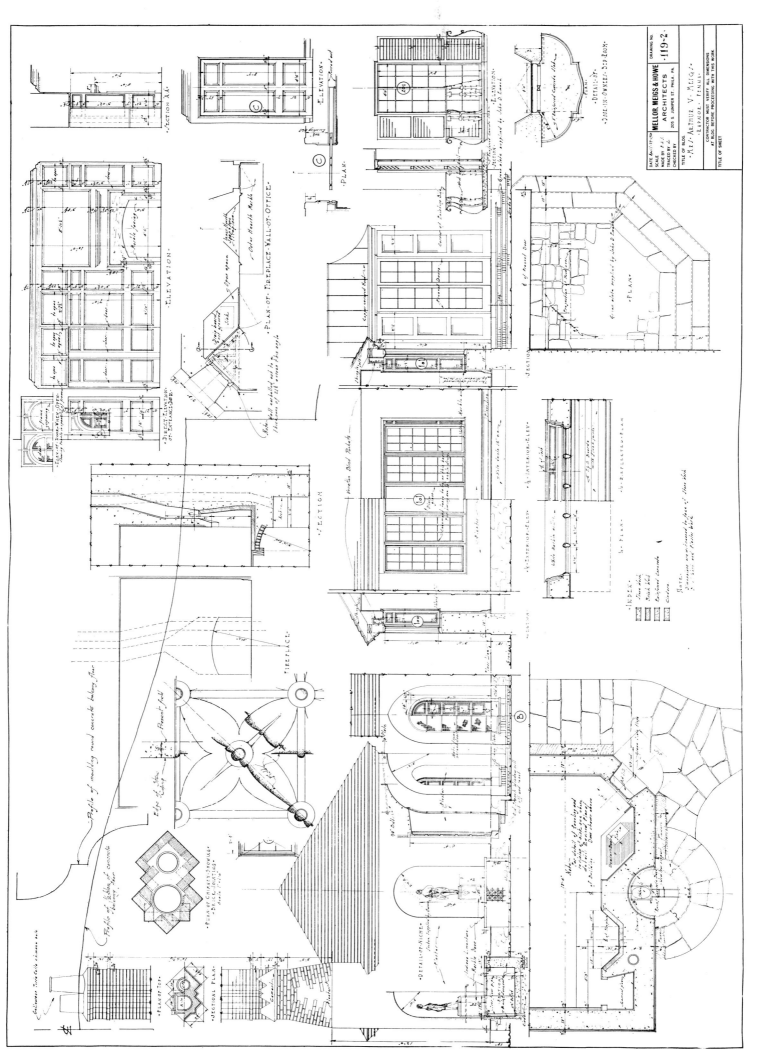

GARDEN ROOM

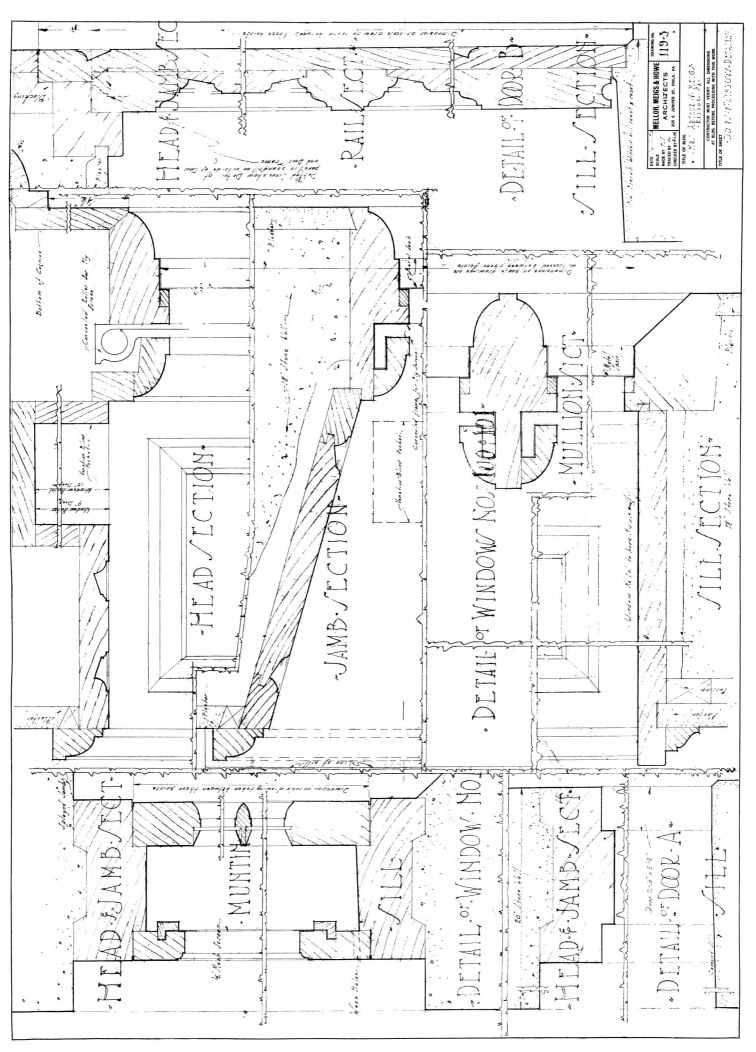

DETAILS OF GARDEN ROOM

JOHN F. MEIGS, II ESQ., RADNOR, PA.

1917

ENTRANCE SIDE

SOUTH EAST FRONT FROM PASTURE

HOUSE FROM THE ROCK GARDEN

BAY IN BED ROOM

FOUNTAIN IN ROCK GARDEN

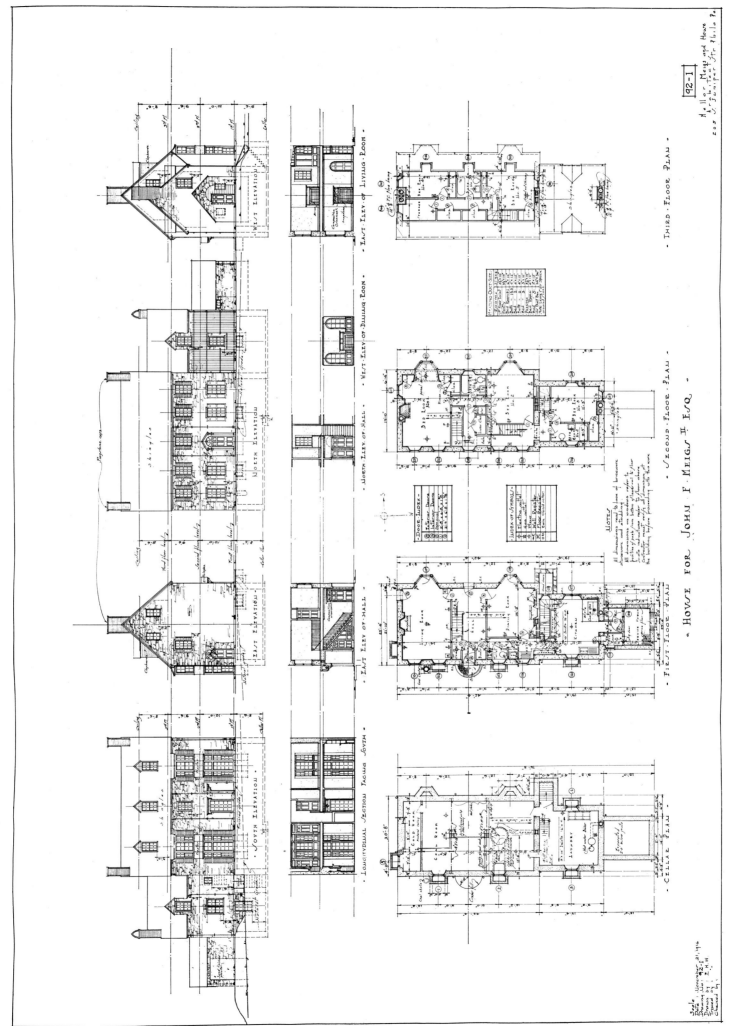

PLANS AND ELEVATIONS

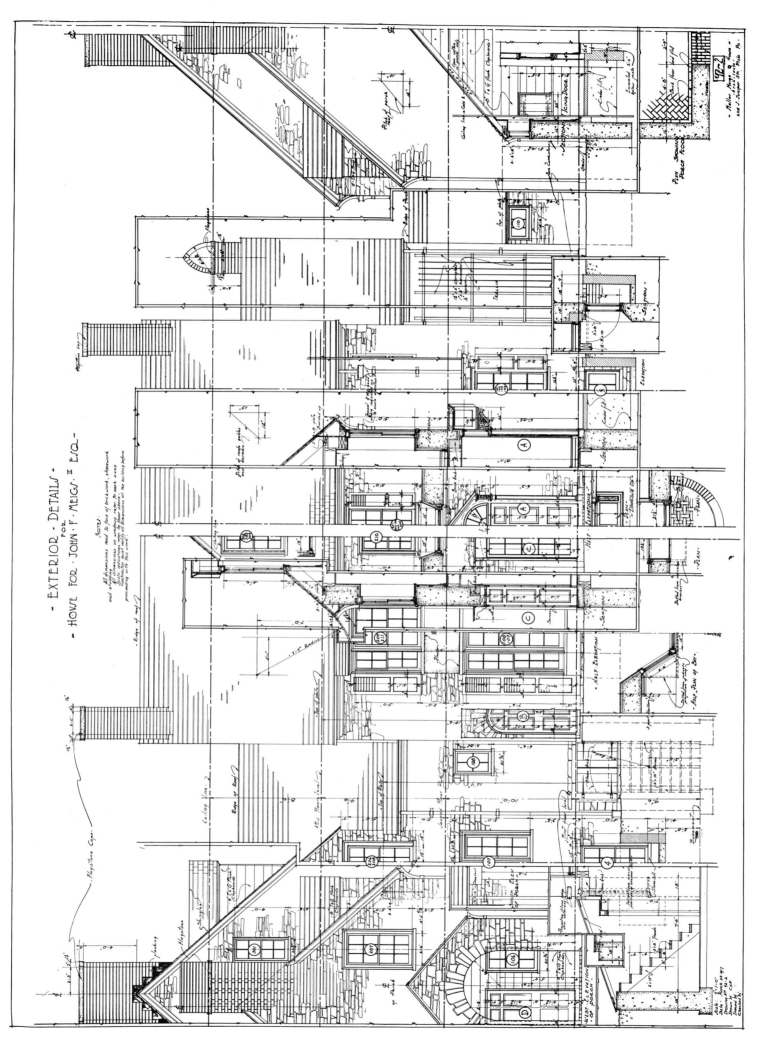

EXTERIOR DETAILS

ENTRANCE SIDE

ENTRANCE SIDE AND SERVICES

HALL TO DINING ROOM

ENTRANCE PASSAGE

WEST SIDE

LIBRARY

SLEEPING PORCH

SECOND STORY HALL

MORNING ROOM FIREPLACE

VAULTED PASSAGE

DINING ROOM

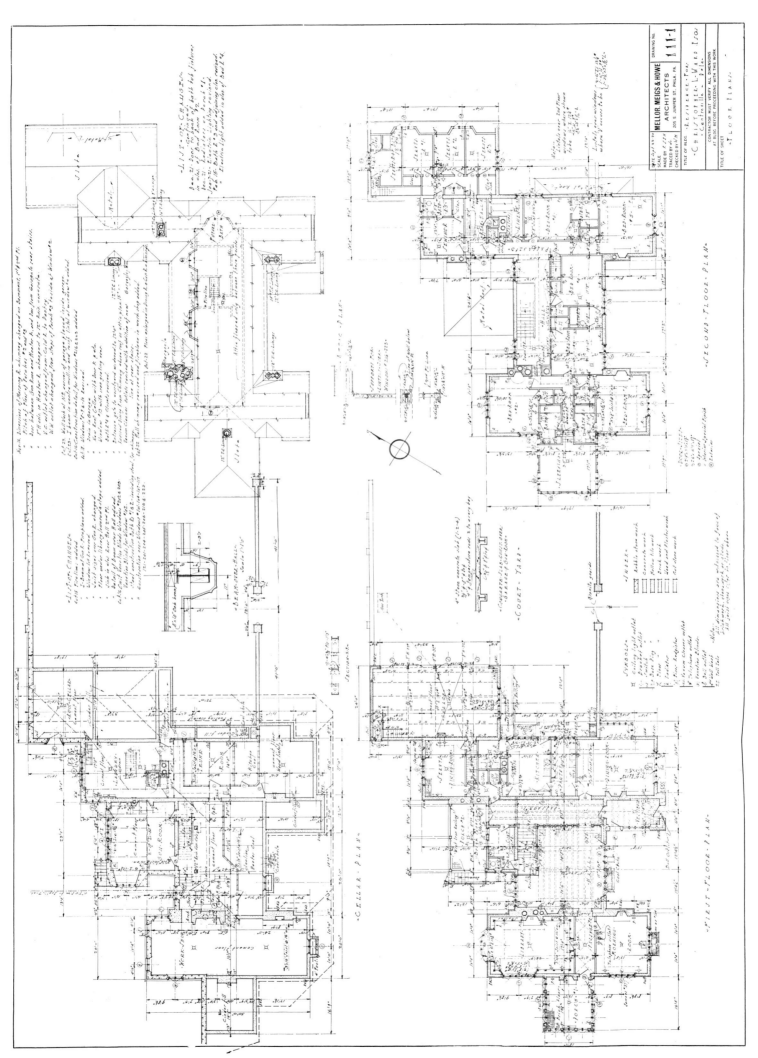

PLANS

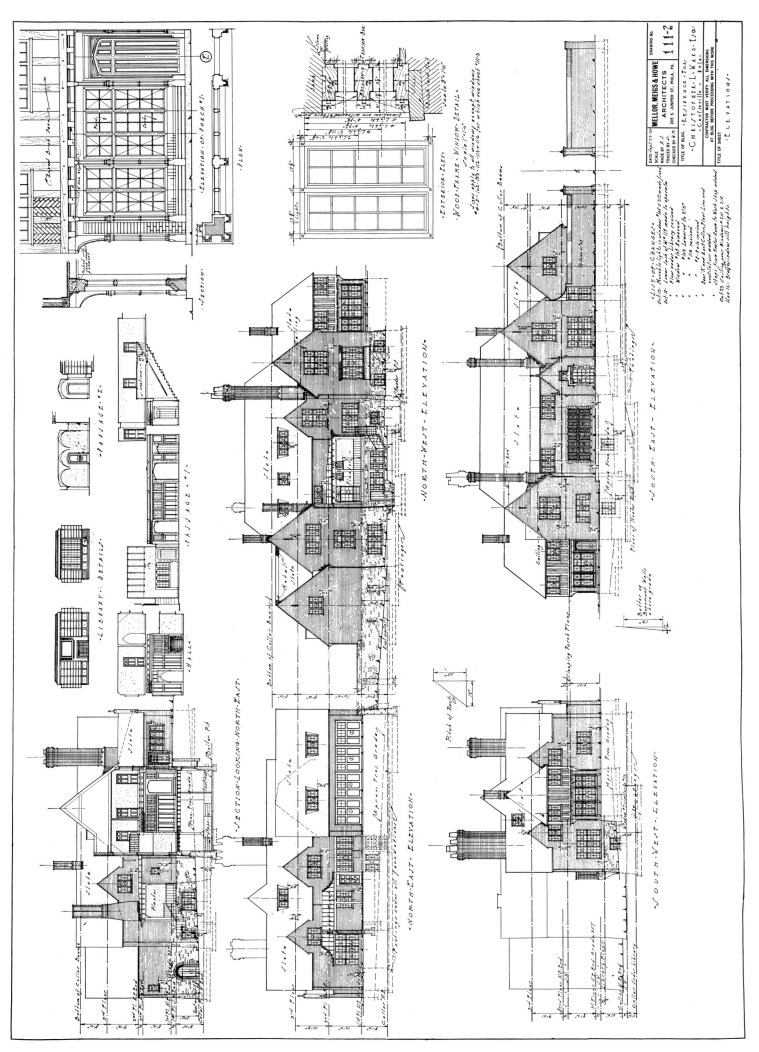

ELEVATIONS

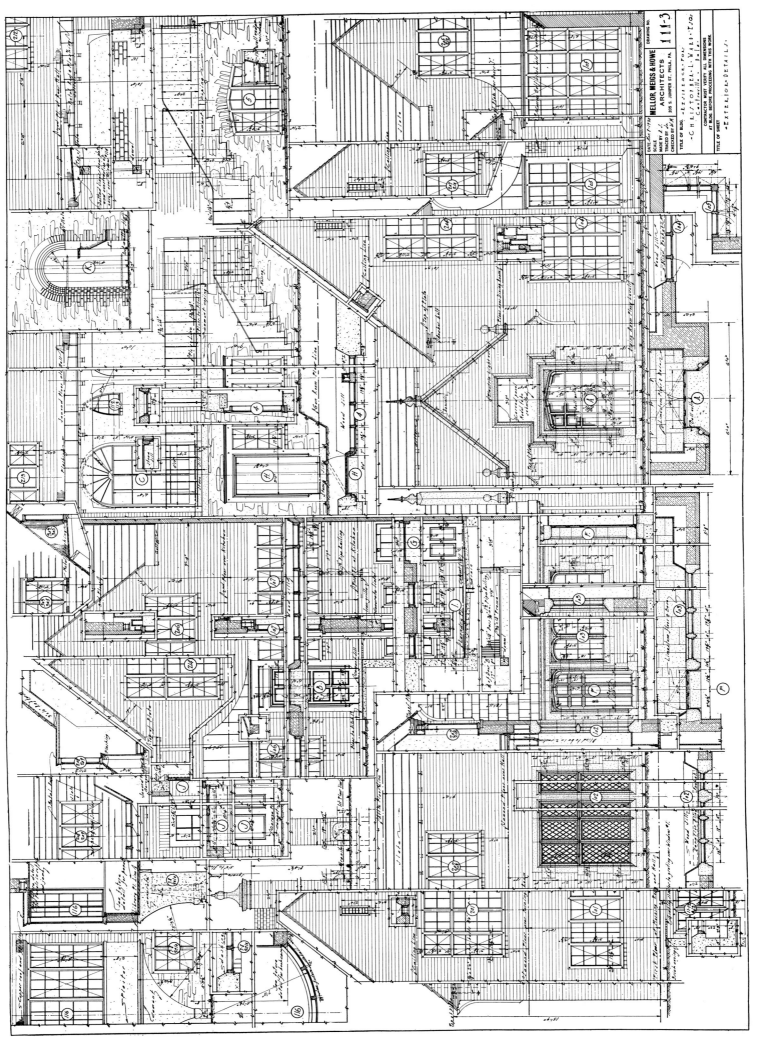

EXTERIOR DETAILS

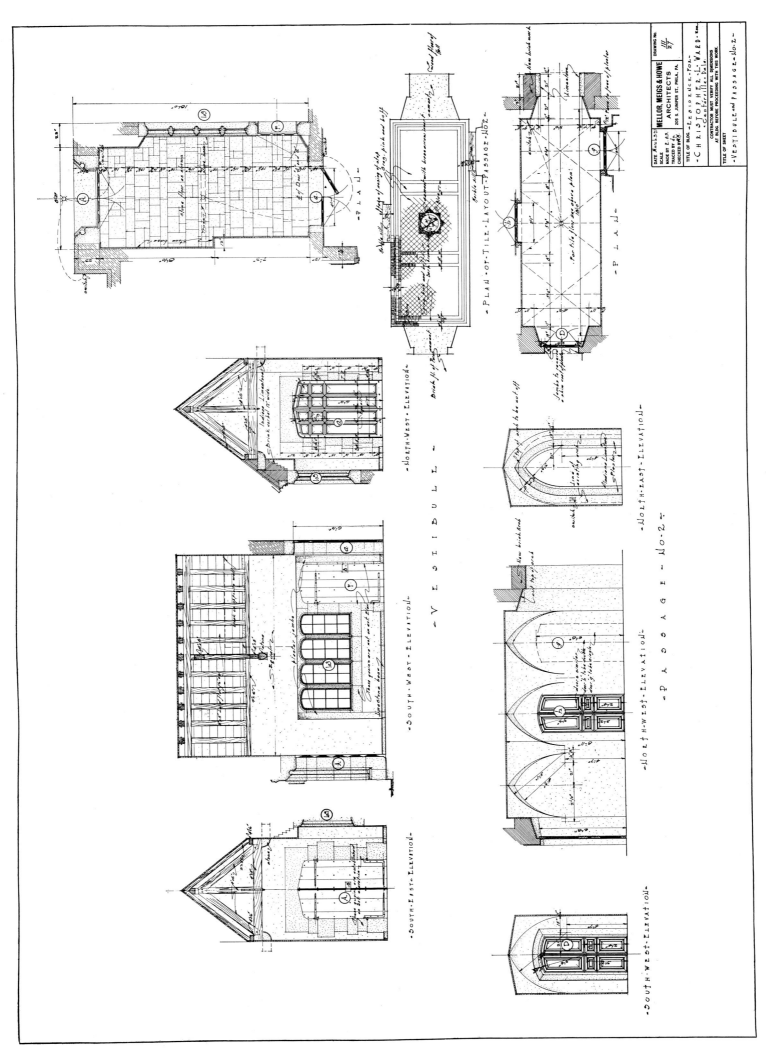

VESTIBULE AND PASSAGE

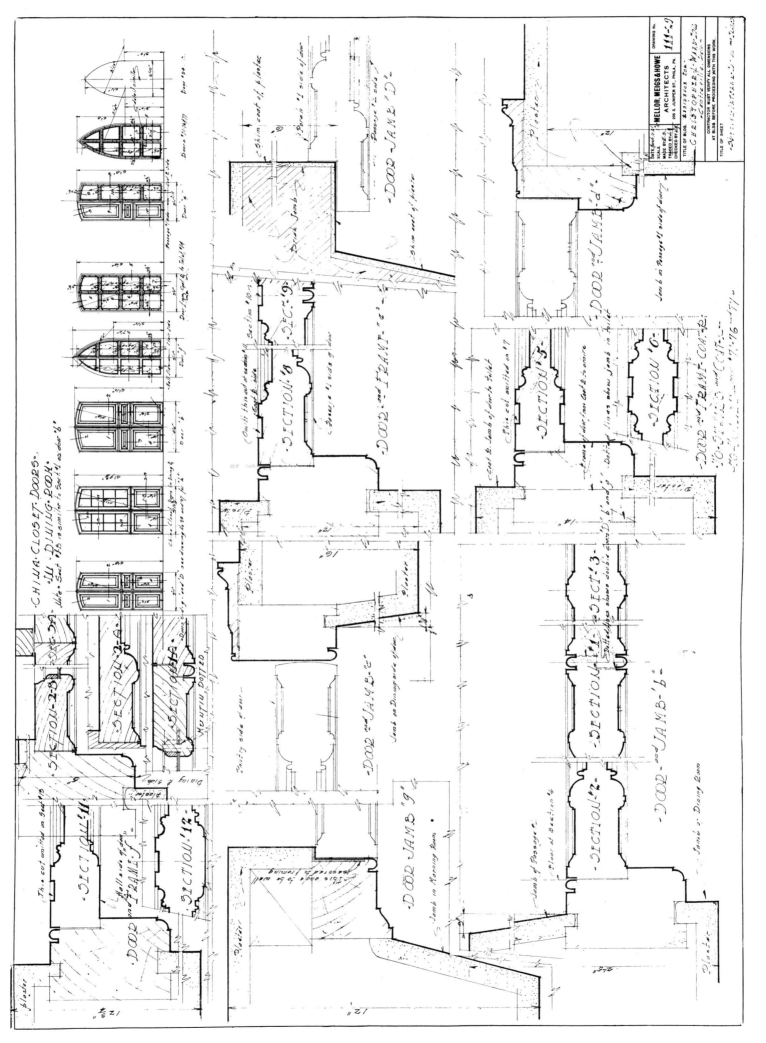

DOORS

ENTRANCE SIDE

PLAN

SEA SIDE

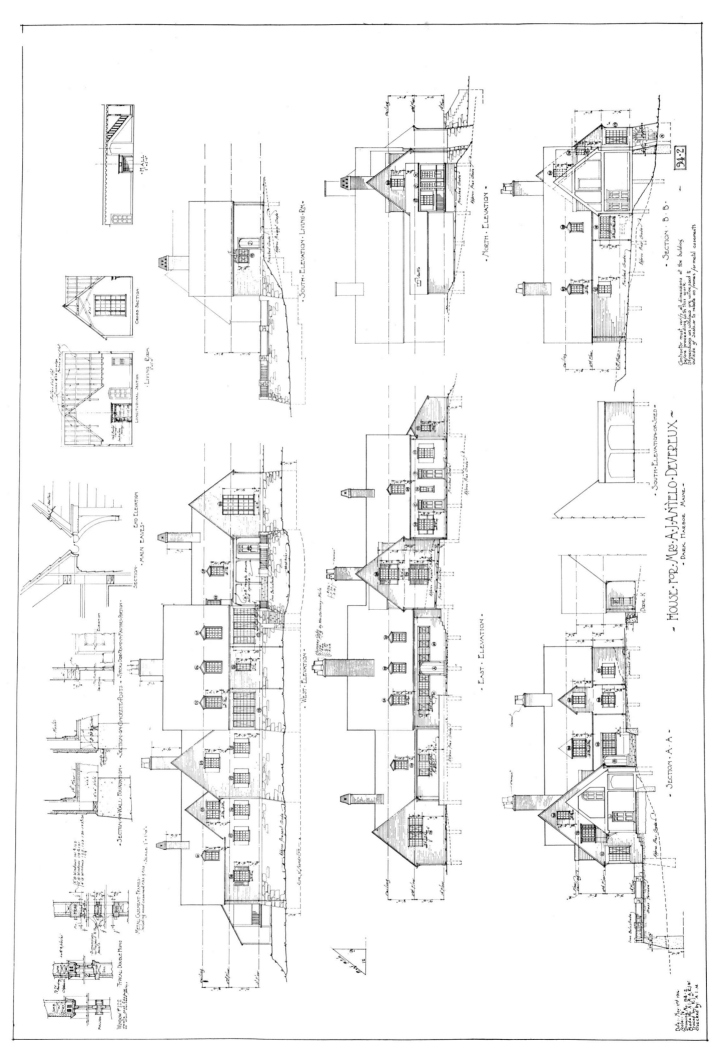

ELEVATIONS

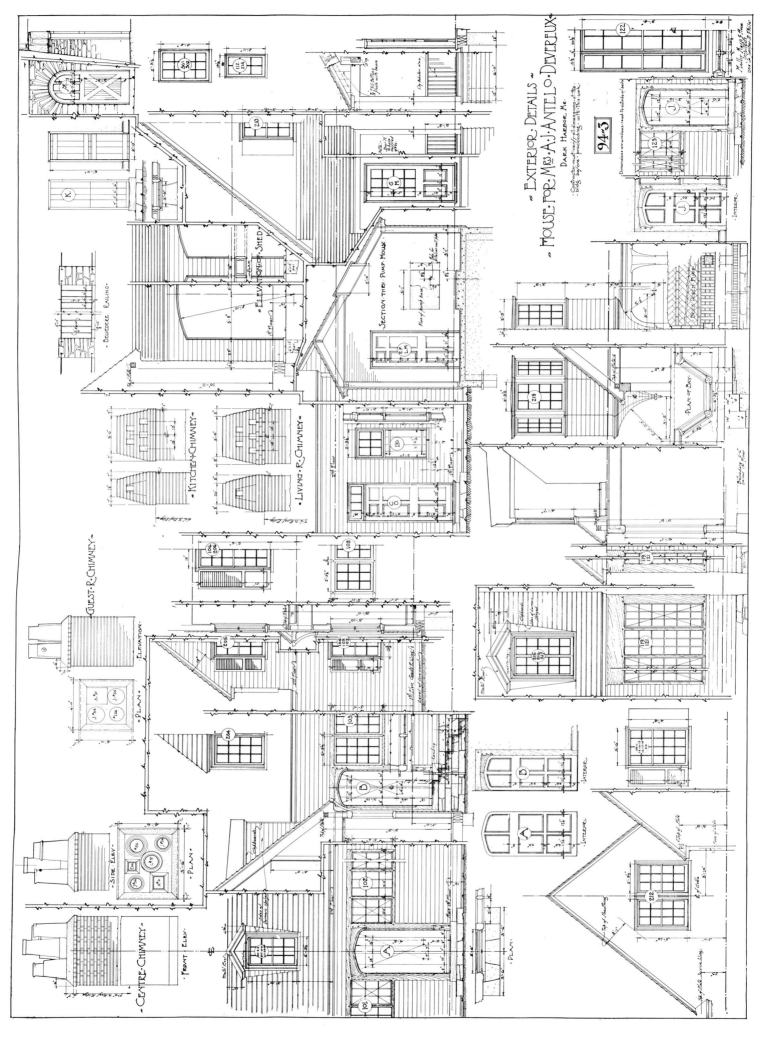

EXTERIOR DETAILS

HOUSE AT CYNWYD, PA.

1911

FROM THE STREET

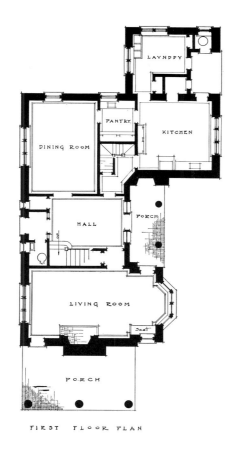

FIRST FLOOR PLAN

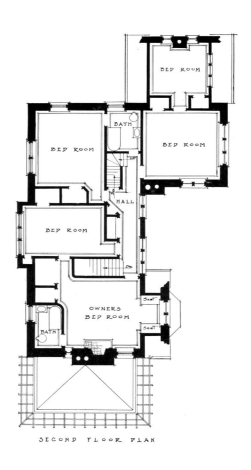

SECOND FLOOR PLAN

PLANS

GARDEN

TWO HOUSES FOR THE MORRIS ESTATE, OVERBROOK, PHILA.

1916

GENERAL VIEW OF BOTH HOUSES

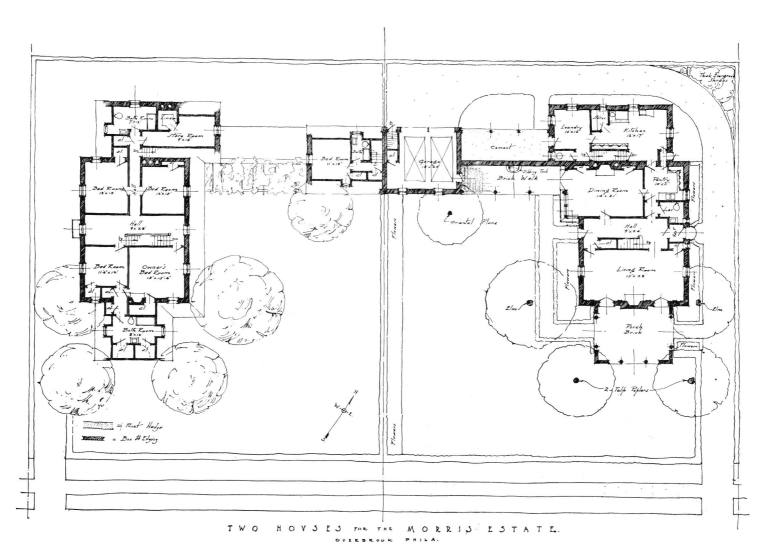

TWO HOUSES FOR THE MORRIS ESTATE, OVERBROOK, PHILA.

PLAN

DINING ROOM BAY FROM WITHOUT

ENTRANCE SIDE

DINING ROOM BAY FROM WITHIN

GARDEN SIDE

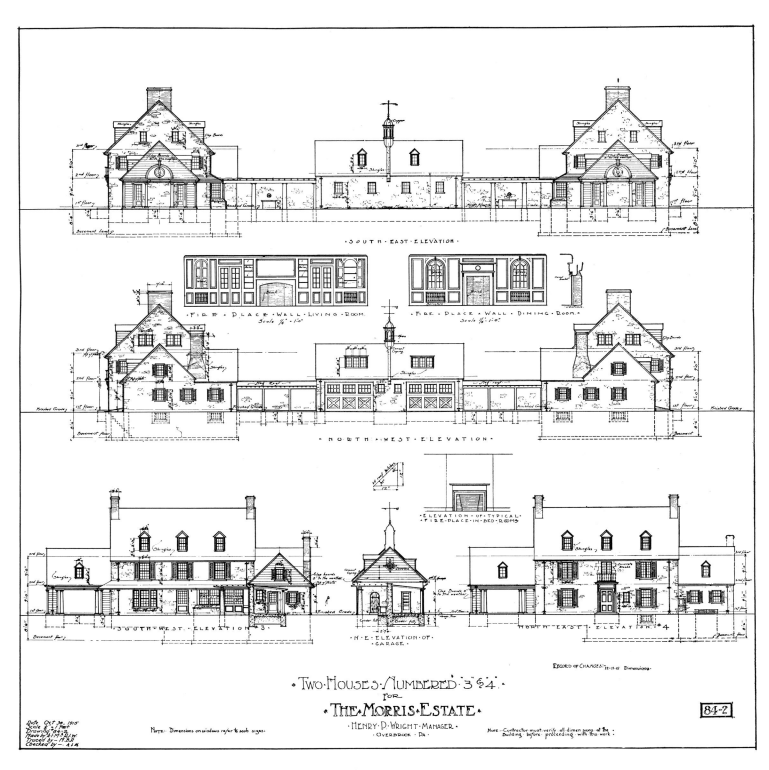

ELEVATIONS

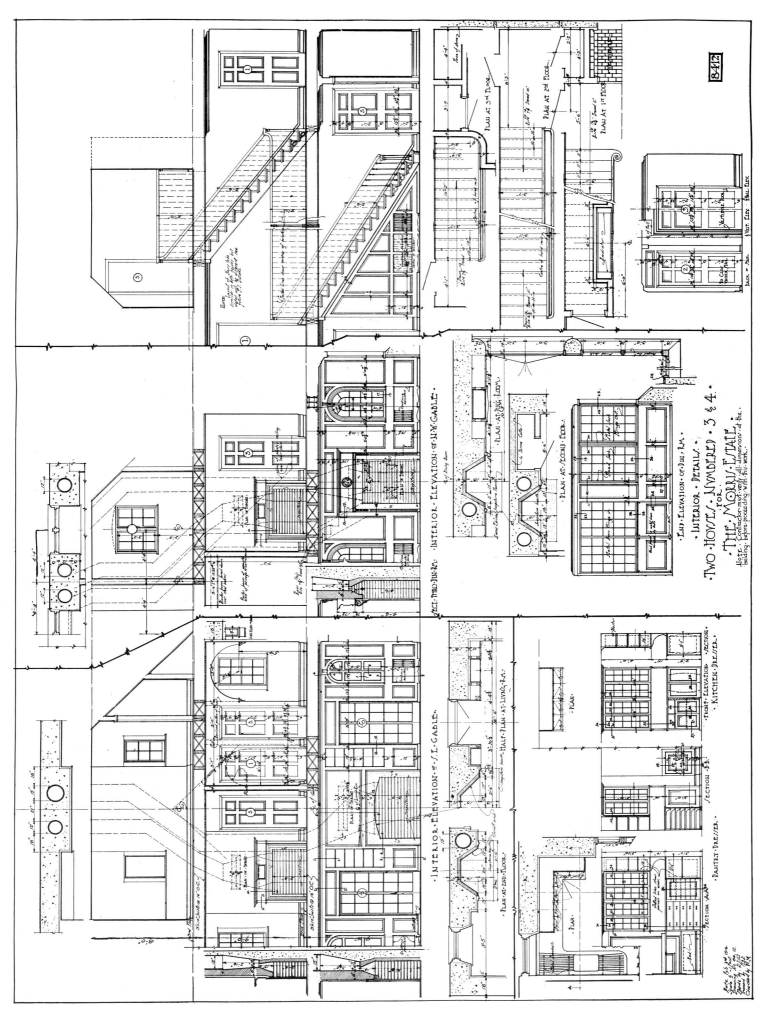

INTERIOR DETAILS

ALTERATIONS AND ADDITIONS TO HOUSE OF ELLIS Y. BROWN, ESQ., DOWNINGTOWN, PA.

1915

ENTRANCE SIDE

SOUTH SIDE

ALTERATIONS AND ADDITIONS TO HOUSE OF ELLIS Y. BROWN, ESQ., DOWNINGTOWN, PA.

1915

ENTRANCE

ALTERATIONS AND ADDITIONS TO HOUSE OF ELLIS Y. BROWN, ESQ., DOWNINGTOWN, PA.

1915

PORCH

DINING ROOM

ALTERATIONS AND ADDITIONS TO HOUSE OF ELLIS Y. BROWN, ESQ., DOWNINGTOWN, PA.

1915

LIVING ROOM

LIVING ROOM FIREPLACE

SECOND STORY HALL

ALTERATIONS AND ADDITIONS TO HOUSE OF ELLIS Y. BROWN, ESQ., DOWNINGTOWN, PA.

1915

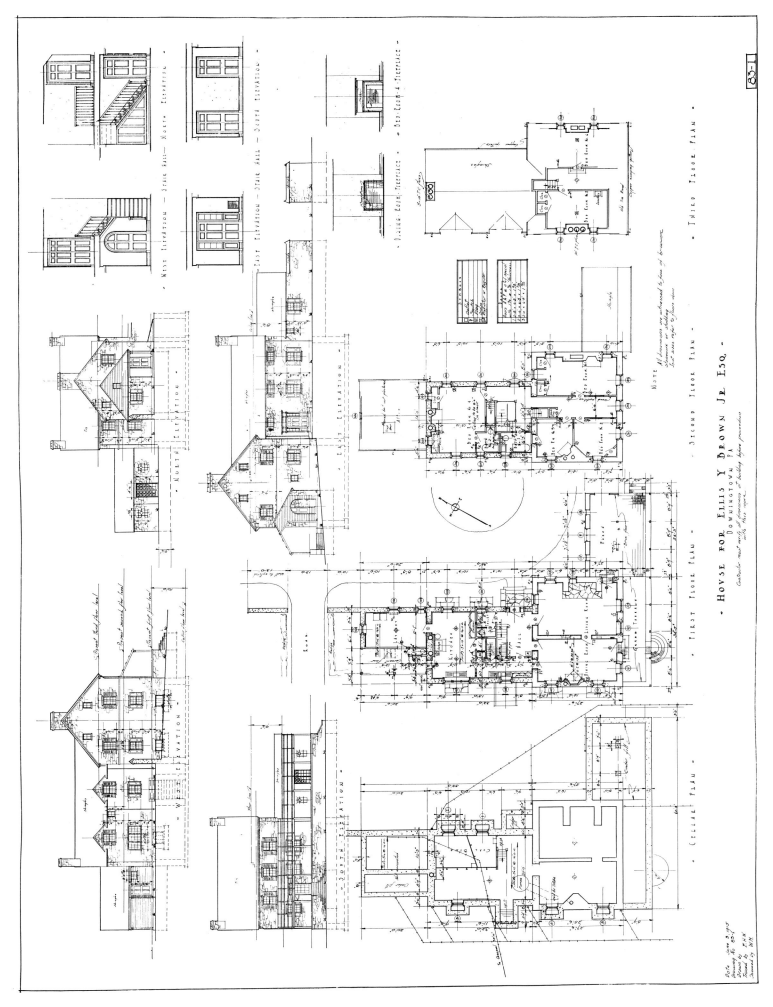

PLANS AND ELEVATIONS

ALTERATIONS AND ADDITIONS TO HOUSE OF ELLIS Y. BROWN, ESQ., DOWNINGTOWN, PA.

1915

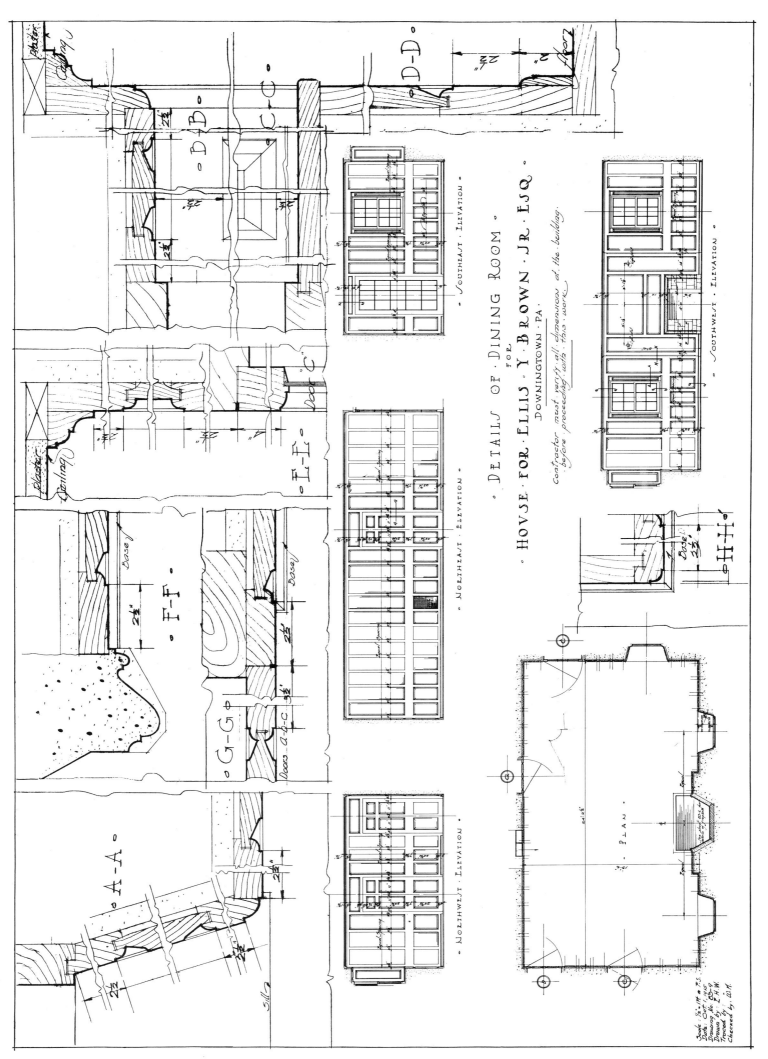

· DETAILS · OF · DINING · ROOM ·
FOR
· HOVSE · FOR · ELLIS · Y · BROWN · JR · ESQ ·
DOWNINGTOWN · PA ·

Contractor must verify all dimensions at the building
before proceeding with this work

DETAILS OF DINING ROOM

FROM LIVING ROOM TO BOOK ROOM

SERVICES

FROM THE PASTURE

SUNKEN GARDEN

FIREPLACE END OF BOOK ROOM

LIVING END OF LIVING AND DINING ROOM

STAIRCASE END OF BOOK ROOM

DINING END OF LIVING AND DINING ROOM

ADDITIONS AND ALTERATIONS IN TWO STAGES TO OLD STABLE OF ALFRED MELLOR, ESQ.

GERMANTOWN—First Alteration, 1909

SIDE VIEW

OLD STABLE

STREET FRONT

ADDITIONS AND ALTERATIONS IN TWO STAGES TO OLD STABLE OF ALFRED MELLOR, ESQ.

GERMANTOWN—First Alteration, 1909

DETAIL OF PORCH

LIVING ROOM

ADDITIONS AND ALTERATIONS IN TWO STAGES TO OLD STABLE OF ALFRED MELLOR, ESQ.

GERMANTOWN—Second Alteration, 1916

FROM THE STREET

ENTRANCE

DETAIL OF LOGGIA

STAIRS

ADDITIONS AND ALTERATIONS IN TWO STAGES TO OLD STABLE OF ALFRED MELLOR, ESQ.

GERMANTOWN—Second Alteration, 1916

LOGGIA FROM STREET

ADDITIONS AND ALTERATIONS IN TWO STAGES TO OLD STABLE OF ALFRED MELLOR, ESQ.

GERMANTOWN

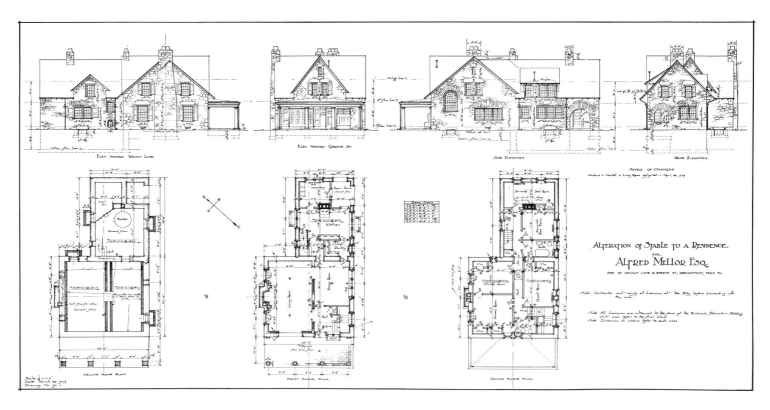

PLANS AND ELEVATIONS
FIRST ALTERATION—1909

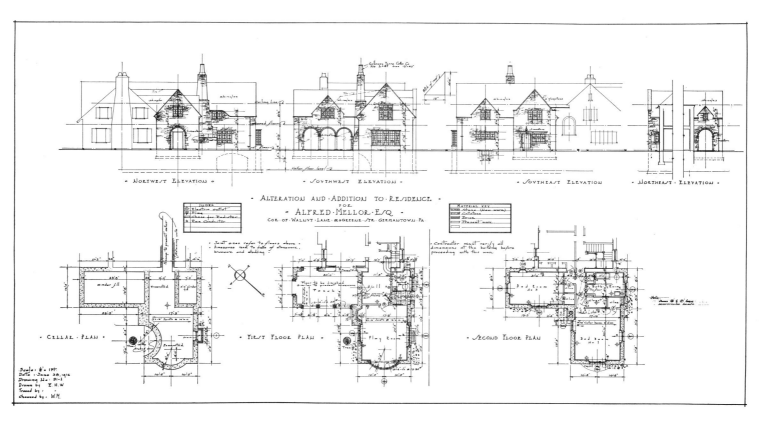

PLANS AND ELEVATIONS
SECOND ALTERATION—1916

FROM THE GARDEN

DINING ROOM

DINING ROOM

PARLOR

FROM THE NORTHWEST

PARLOR FIREPLACE

FROM THE STREET

PRINCETON CHARTER CLUB, PRINCETON, N. J.

1913

ENTRANCE TERRACE

ENTRANCE

LIBRARY

CLUB ROOM

FIRST FLOOR HALL

STAIRS

SECOND FLOOR HALL

DINING ROOM FIREPLACE

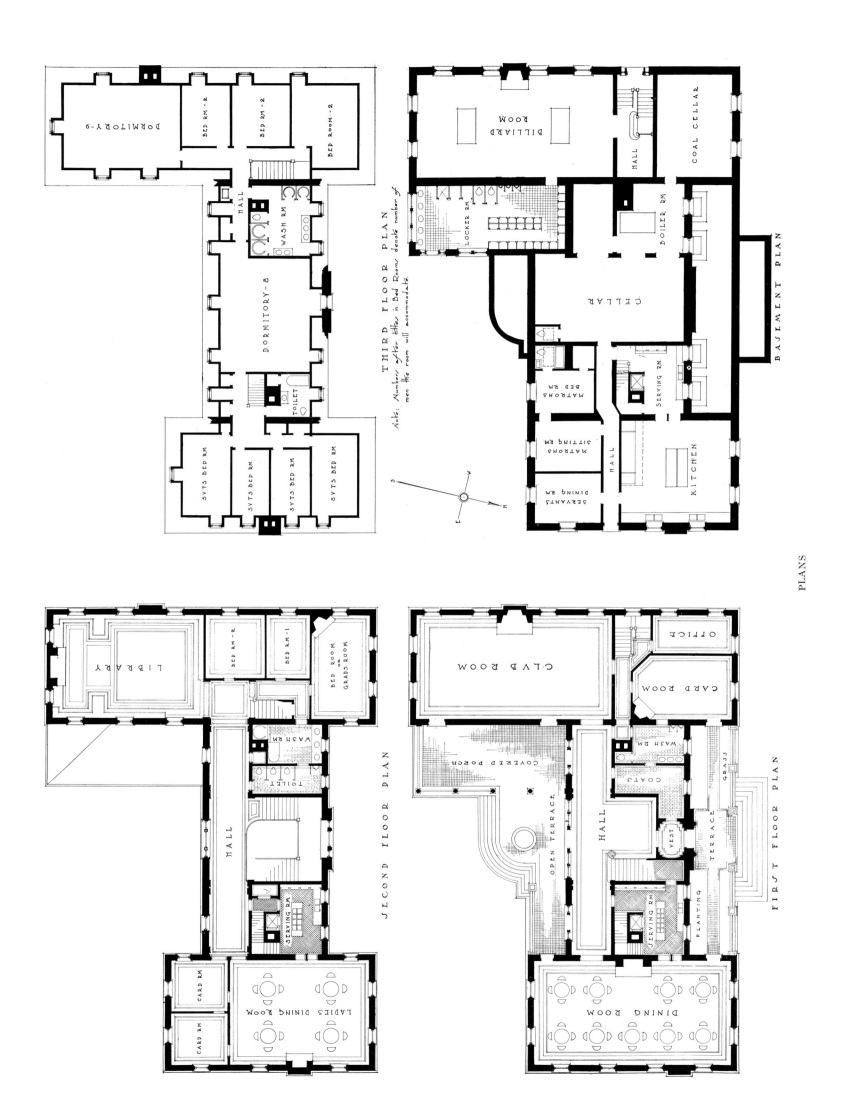

THIRD FLOOR PLAN

Note: Numbers after titles in Bed Rooms denote number of men the room will accommodate.

BASEMENT PLAN

SECOND FLOOR PLAN

FIRST FLOOR PLAN

PLANS

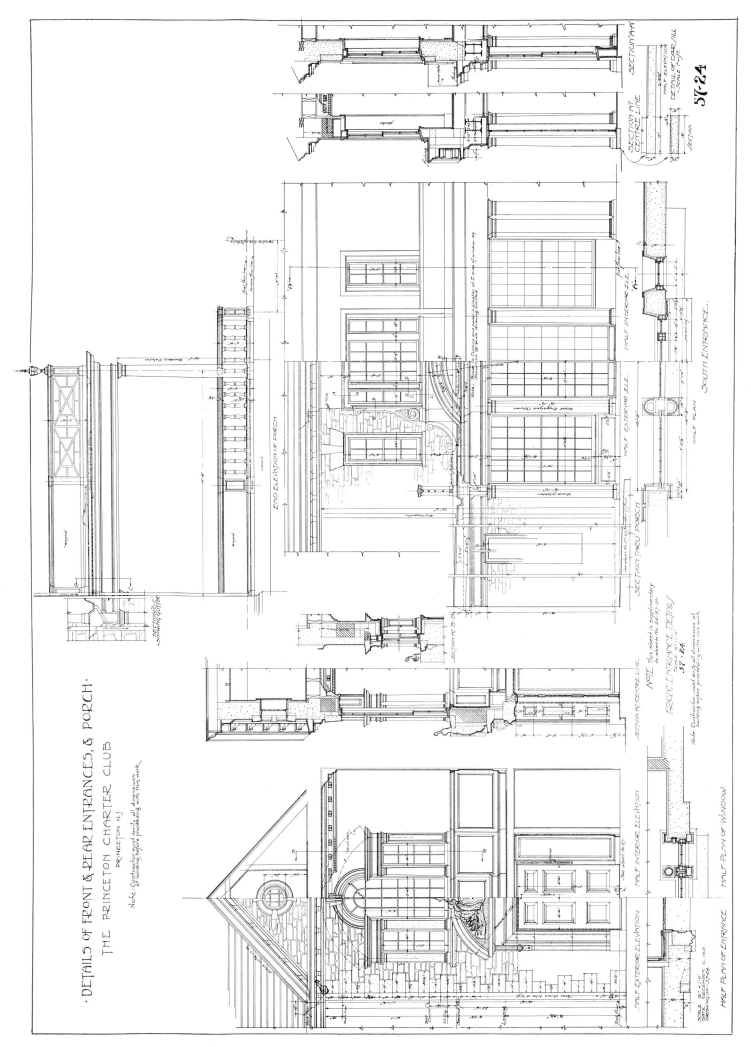

EXTERIOR DETAILS

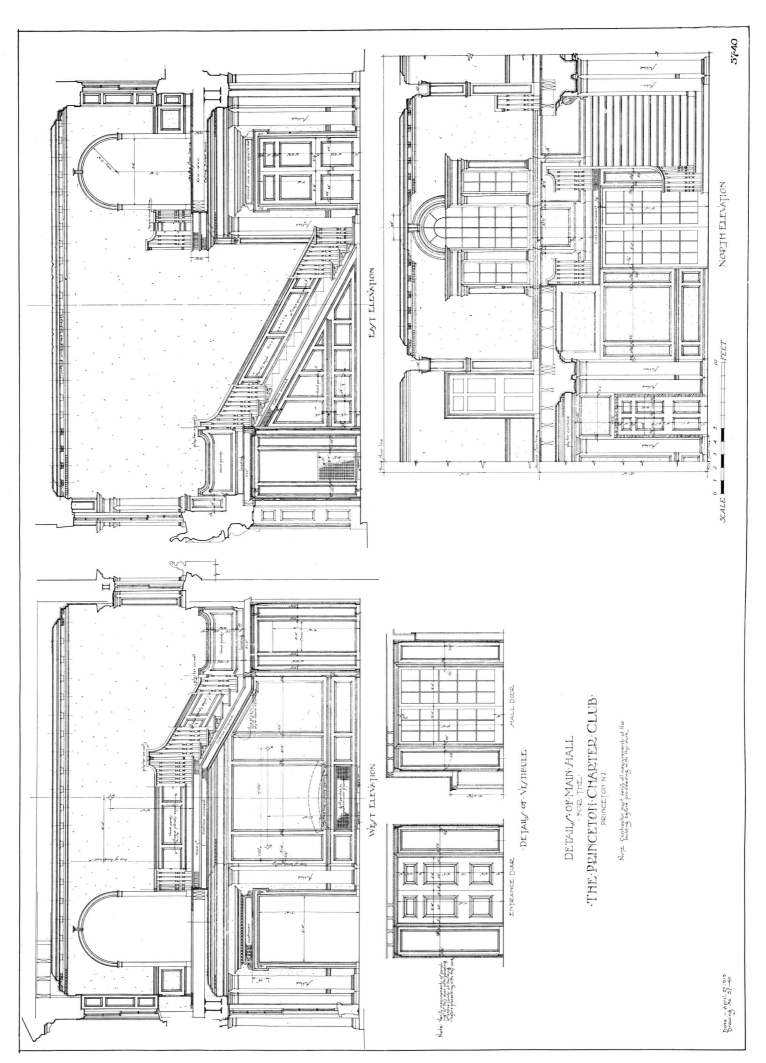

PHI GAMMA DELTA FRATERNITY HOUSE, UNIVERSITY OF PENNSYLVANIA, PHILA.

1914

FRONT

PHI GAMMA DELTA FRATERNITY HOUSE, UNIVERSITY OF PENNSYLVANIA, PHILA.

1914

ENTRANCE

FROM THE SOUTHWEST

PHI GAMMA DELTA FRATERNITY HOUSE, UNIVERSITY OF PENNSYLVANIA, PHILA.

1914

STAIRS

VESTIBULE

HALL SCREEN

DINING ROOM SIDEBOARD

GALLERY IN CLUB ROOM

PHI GAMMA DELTA FRATERNITY HOUSE, UNIVERSITY OF PENNSYLVANIA, PHILA.

1914

HALL

TOWARDS CLUB ROOM

GALLERY AND MANTEL IN CLUB ROOM

DINING ROOM

CLUB ROOM

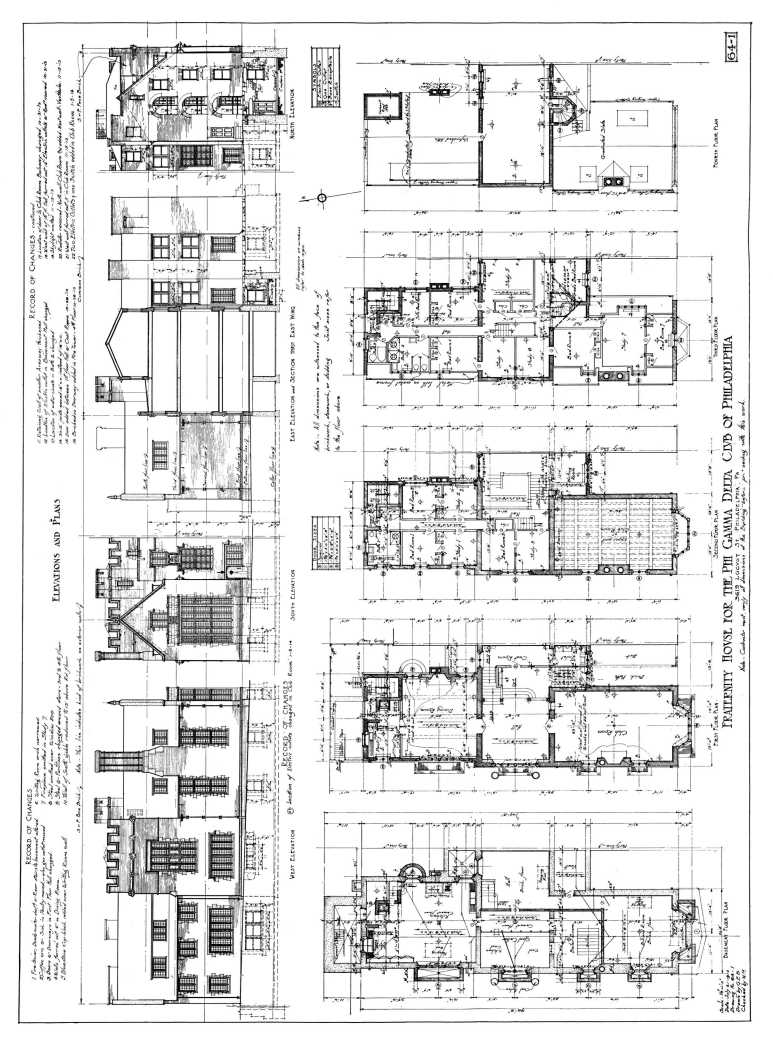

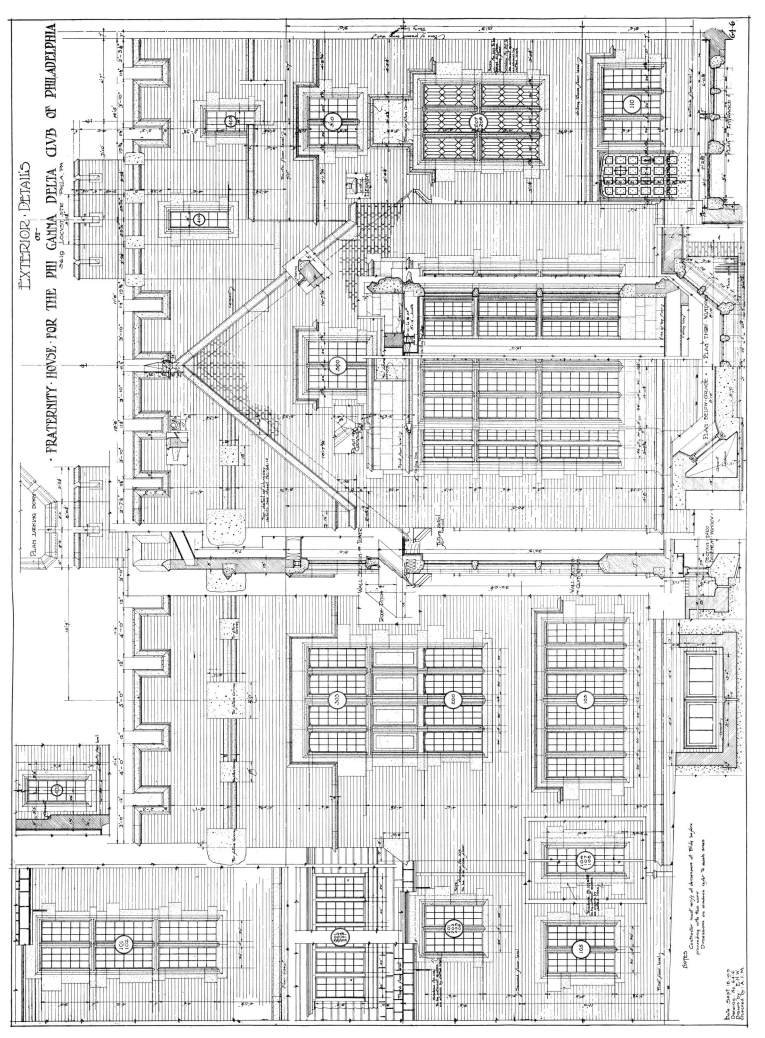

EXTERIOR DETAILS

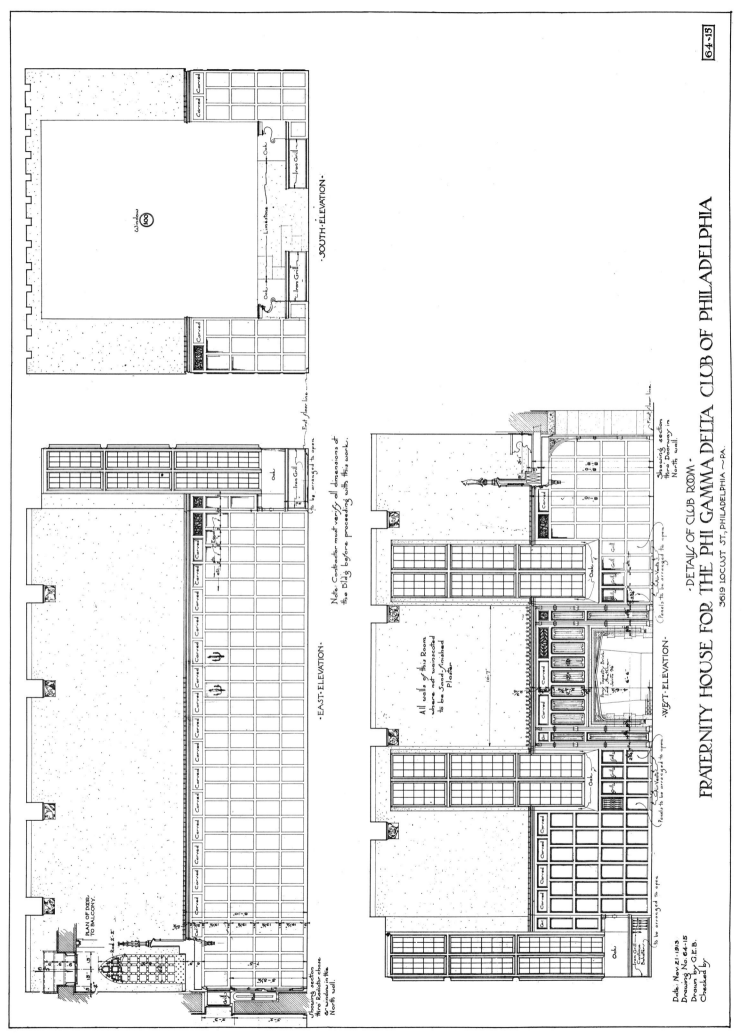

FRATERNITY HOUSE FOR THE PHI GAMMA DELTA CLUB OF PHILADELPHIA

3619 LOCUST ST, PHILADELPHIA — PA.

CLUB ROOM

ENTRANCE

OLD WAGON SHED MADE INTO PORCH

SOUTH TERRACE

PICKERING HUNT CLUB, PHOENIXVILLE, PA.

1911

FROM THE SOUTHWEST

HALL AND DINING ROOM FROM CLUB ROOM

MEN'S DORMITORY

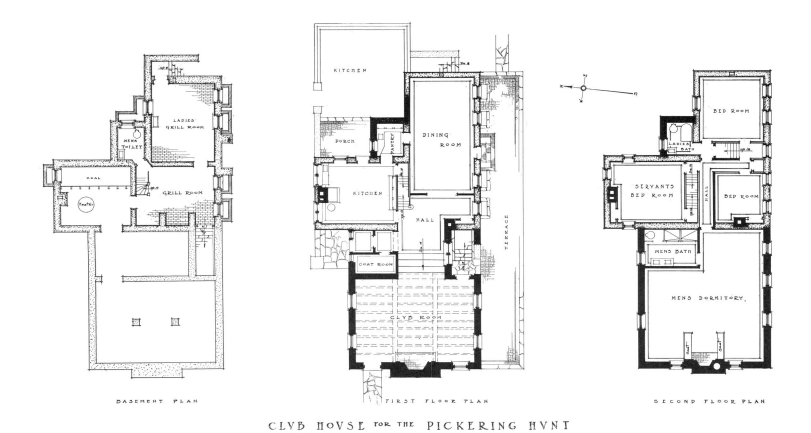

CLVB HOVSE FOR THE PICKERING HVNT

PHOENIXVILLE PA.

PLANS

(An alteration to an old Farm House; black portion is new)

FOUR BUILDINGS

The Bird House of the Philadelphia Zoological Society
The Workshop of Mr. Samuel Yellin
The Garden Building of Charles Biddle, Esq.
The Office of Messrs. Mellor, Meigs & Howe.

THOUGH the four buildings, or groups of buildings, shown in the illustrations which follow this article, serve varied ends, from the hardest work to the lightest play, they possess one characteristic in common—each in its separate field is the outcome of an agreeable human necessity.

The importance of this characteristic cannot be over-estimated. Human necessity is the seed from which springs architectural design, and by necessity design is foreordained, not only in its general outline, but in its every detail, as the form and feature of a plant are determined before the first shoot has burst its sheath. Furthermore, as a plant will inevitably develop some special and satisfying quality—if not the fragrance of the rose or the strength of the oak, at least the humble succulence of the cabbage—if allowed to follow its natural development from the seed, unwarped and unblighted, so will every building develop some special and satisfying quality, however humble it may be, if allowed to follow its inevitable growth from the seed of human necessity. This special and satisfying quality constitutes the essential beauty of a building as of a plant, and on this essential beauty the by-product of mere external beauty is utterly dependent. To develop the finest rose or the argest head of cabbage, the horticulturist does not study the convolutions and veinings of the leaves and petals, but examines in each kind of plant its essential characteristics and needs, seeking to develop the former and meet the latter; nor, if he be wise, will he attempt to cross the strains of the rose and the cabbage, even though the bloom of the one somewhat resemble in form the head of the other. In the same way, the most perfect specimens of any species of buildings can be developed only by nurturing and maturing the characteristics inherent in the inevitable necessities, both material and spiritual, of the species to which the buildings belong, and not by studying how they may be transferred from one species to another. In this way that essential beauty will be obtained of which external beauty is the by-product, more or less fortuitous and subject to the whims of fashion.

I may seem to have dwelt over-long on this horticultural simile, which is intended to demonstrate the organic nature of architecture, for, it will be said, the halls of our schools of design resound, and the pages of our technical publications are black, with the word "organic," and with lengthy dissertations on its meaning. Yet I must continue to emphasize the importance of the dictates of organic growth in architecture, which, however much they may be respected in theory, are ever more honored in the breach than in the observance when it comes to practice. This state of affairs is due to an unwillingness on the part of architect and public alike to recognize the inexorable fact that an architectural plant, like its natural prototype, grows from a seed over which we have no control, or at least only such control as LUTHER BURBANK may exercise over his specimens by the process of artificial selection and hybridization, which can be practised successfully only within certain limits. We cannot grow oaks from cabbage seed, nor roses from acorns, yet the public constantly demands such conjuring tricks of the architect, and he in turn, in order not to disappoint his audience, and perhaps himself ignorant of the iniquity of the deception he is practising, seeks to produce from an incongruous seed some faint semblance of the desired plant by distorting the real growth, by wiring its members to maintain them in strange postures and looping about it festoons of artificial leaves and flowers of his own manufacture. The result of his labors, however ingeniously deceptive to the eye, cannot but incite ridicule when the deception is discovered, as do those realistic shadow pictures of the Crucifix with which over-zealous European monks have adorned the walls of so many of their refectories.

It is not my intention, nor will the scope of the present article allow me to enter on a lengthy analysis of the manifestions of the architectural conjuring tricks and deceptions I have outlined. Suffice it to cite, as an example of those festoons of artificial leaves and flowers to which I have alluded, the architectural forms and adornments, classic, mediaeval and modern, which are wired to the metal limbs of our halls of commerce—adornments borrowed from the pyramids, temples, churches, belfries and spires of bygone times. They are manifestly not a natural and organic growth, either from the spirit or fabric of the buildings they adorn, and therefore, though they may momentarily deceive the eye and mind by their superficial beauty, a nearer examination will disclose that they are as little expressive of the essence of the civilization on which they are superimposed as the Chapel of St. Hubert at Amboise is expressive of a suburban garage. If the Chapel of St. Hubert were reproduced by some new Croesus for the purpose of storing his automobiles, the world would resound with mocking laughter, even though the reproduction were ten times more beautiful than the original; yet when Mr. Woolworth dresses up the spirit of his Five and Ten Cent Store in the garments of mediaeval mysticism, the world stands in awed and admiring silence, and with head uncovered, before the anomalous and ridiculous spectacle. I have chosen the Woolworth Building with intention, as one of the most beautiful examples of its type, in order to accentuate the fact that its superficial beauty is as nothing when weighed in the balance against its fundamental falsity, and that until this falsity is recognized and a new method of approach to modern architectural problems is sought, no real progress can be made. This method must closely approximate that of the horticulturist. We must study more deeply our special seeds of human necessity, material and spiritual, in order that we may develop buildings with that fine organic quality which is the only true beauty, and shun not only ridiculous artifices, but also that hybridization between different species which, in art as in nature, produces sterility. We must recognize that nature intended that there should be cabbages in architecture as in the vegetable kingdom, and develop the essential quality of the cabbage to its highest possibilities, instead of attempting to disguise it. Cabbages are stately enough when planted in orderly rows, decently weeded, whereas artificial flowers are an absurdity not to be tolerated.

I have used the four buildings which we began to consider in the first paragraph of this article as a quadruple peg on which to hang the garment of my architectural homily because, however humble they may be, it is possible to trace in their varied forms the natural growth of which I have been speaking. I have said that each of them sprang from an agreeable human necessity—that is to say that the seed was of a nature to produce a fragrant flower. Whether the architectural result be beautiful or not is of little moment, since it is my only purpose to examine with a scientific eye the connection between its outward manifestations and its deep-rooted functions, and not to pass judgment on such technical matters as style, proportion, or color.

Without entering into the subject of why human beings collect birds it may be said, without fear of contradiction, that the purpose of a bird-house is to show them, and in designing the Bird House at the Philadelphia Zoological Gardens everything was subordinated to this central idea. Birds are in themselves a decoration and need only a pleasant background against which to group themselves in order to form a succession of pictures of such amazing variety and color as no mural painting can equal. No effort is made, therefore, to provide in the birds' surroundings any simulation of nature, such as sometimes serves in zoological gardens as a dreary reminder that the animals are in captivity, but the indoor and outdoor cages (the latter surrounding the walls of the two wings) are built against a plain wall of gray-buff plaster on which every color tells like an accent. Over the outdoor cages rows of trees spread their shade, and provide in Summer some semblance of the play of light in a forest in which the birds shine at their natural best.

In order to give the building that architectural aspect from a distance which it could not have had had it been treated only as a background for the birds, the large central space containing the flying cage is expressed on the exterior as a loggia, the only important architectural adornment. This again was suggested by the subject. The architects' desire to bring together the birds of land and water had controlled the location of the building near the lake, though it had been the original intention of the Directors of the Zoological Society to place it elsewhere. The lake in its turn suggested the classic device of architecture reflected in water, and the deep shadow of the loggia was designed to give full value to this effect.

The details are in character with the lightness and featheriness of the birds. The arch is high-sprung to express flight and the columns are as tenuous as the legs of the flamingo himself. The capitals of the columns are ornamented with feathery acanthus leaves, and the spandrils with panels of turkey gobblers, while in the arch a macaw of glazed terra-cotta, in full color, sits suspended on his swing under a painted vault of leaves and golden sky in which more of his feathered brethren are poised. Good or bad the design of the Bird House may at least be said to have grown naturally from its inevitable purposes.

With the Bird House may be classed the Gate House of the Zoological Gardens, standing in close proximity, and having for its principal adornment the wrought-iron entrance and exit gates and the shelter over the ticket-seller's window, all ineluctable necessities, and all by the hand of Mr. Yellin.

While the Bird House is an outcome of humanity's more playful humor Mr. Yellin's Workshop is an expression of the necessity of work. Yet work is tempered by play in the workshop of the artificer in iron, for though the forge is a hard taskmaster it yet gives the spirit and imagination of the artisan free play, while it exercises his skilful and sinewy hands. As in the case of the Bird House, the problem resolves itself into a research in background—a background for the owner's craftsmanship—and the plan is the extreme of simplicity. The building stands on a city lot bounded by streets on two sides, and divides itself naturally into two parts of which the smaller, or front part, contains the offices, and the larger part in the rear contains the innumerable forges and the small amount of machinery. The working portion may be disposed of briefly by saying that it is frankly a factory, has the largest possible area of glass in its walls and is "adorned" with no glazed brick, terra-cotta, cast stone or other architectural "features." The office portion is treated, inside and out, as a background for the work of the owner, than which no better expression of the building's purpose, or means of decorating it, could be found. As the photographs will show, the walls and doors are plain and accentuate the lines and shadows of the ornamental iron-work which varies their monotony. The openings have deep reveals and are arranged in every case in such a way as to throw the gates and grilles into relief, either in dark on light or light on dark. In no case was the plan distorted to attain this object, but the idea of iron-work was kept always in mind. The thought was to allow the human necessity of the building to express itself, rather than to give it expression. The greater part of the iron-work was designed by the owner, though a few details were made by the architects, and no other architectural device was introduced save a brick base, a parapet pierced with cylindrical tiles, and an ornamental treatment of the arch and lintel on the *pan coupe*, all of which were kept in a character to express the simplicity of the workshop and the rugged nature of the work carried on therein.

The third of the buildings we are considering is again the outcome of a playful need. There is no type of architecture which gives freer rein to the imagination than the outbuildings of a country place. Their form and feature are often not determined by specific needs, but only by a general need for more room, the spaces are generous and the requirements of light are not excessive, so that it is possible to arrange the silhouette, fenestration and wall spaces almost as fancy may dictate. The Garden Building of Mr. Biddle is no exception. Yet the freedom of treatment which the subject permits is in itself a danger, like the length of the proverbial rope by which the wrong-doer is supposed to hang himself. The architect's only certain guide is the character of the place of which the outbuildings form a part—in this case, as the photographs indicate, a farm. The building is in part a restoration, while another portion serves as a residence, both of which considerations served in a great measure to establish the form of the group, while the desire to complete the frame of the garden was the final factor in determining the design. The portion which serves as a residence has a full third floor at one point, forming a tower, which is provided with an outside staircase communicating with the garden, at whose angle a strong "buttress" is formed with these elements, while by their introduction the practical plan of the residence is improved. The other portion of the buildings serves as a store-house, and is treated with very few openings, to form a high wall at one end of the garden. In this way, without any "architectural" tricks, a picturesque group is formed, which at the same time meets all the practical requirements for which the building is intended.

The necessities governing the design of the fourth building, we are considering, an architect's office, are sufficiently obvious to need no explanation. An architect must have light, he must have an office space and a working space, and (if he be interested in anything beyond plumbing fixtures) he must have a place to cogitate—a space sufficiently inspiring to distract his thoughts from the goading detail of modern construction. Out of these necessities has grown the office of Mellor, Meigs and Howe. The space devoted to the work of the members of the firm is also dedicated to that necessary cogitation aforementioned, and dominates the design. It is not large in area, but lofty and well-lit, rising to the rafters and roof-tree, and capped by a lantern. It dominates the design both in importance and bulk, and expresses the human necessity on which so much stress has been laid; while the other portions of the plan, as the photographs show, fall into their natural and subordinate places.

From a consideration of these four buildings, far apart in external appearance but all governed by the same considerations of inevitable necessity in design, it may be seen how meaningless are those considerations of "style" and "taste" on which so much stress is laid today. Whether the buildings be thought beautiful or ugly by this individual or that, or by the architects themselves, is of no moment, if they have grown of necessity from a vital seed, and whether they be rag-weed or orchid matters not, if they fitly fulfill their predestined end.

And now, ungentle reader, you have perhaps been laughing in your sleeve that I should attempt to draw so important a lesson from four buildings so insignificant in bulk and value. Yet I have chosen them as my text for a reason that should change your laughter to tears; I have chosen them because the agreeable human necessities from which they have grown, and on which I have laid such stress, have become so rare in our commercial era that the least token of their presence must be noted and cherished. Whatever quality these buildings may possess springs in the first instance from the presence of these same agreeable necessities, without which the architect is helpless to clothe his buildings in that outward grace which has distinguished the highest type of architecture in all ages. Do not misunderstand me to mean that grace is the quality which makes architecture great; it is but a necessary adjunct of the highest type of greatness, in architecture as in man, and as in man so in architecture it is worthless, nay worse, if it be no more than an outward affectation. The agreeable human necessities of which grace is the expression in architecture must become a reality in the spirit of the community before the architect can seek in them a vital and living inspiration for the adornment of the mere fabric of his buildings. Here and there, among the few, agreeable human necessities exist, and find architectural voice. Among the many they are still confused with creature comfort and material prosperity, of which our most imposing buildings are the expression, clothed in a borrowed grace.

GEORGE HOWE.

BIRD HOUSE FOR THE PHILADELPHIA ZOOLOGICAL GARDENS

1915

CENTRAL PAVILION

ENTRANCE

SOUTH GATE OF GARDENS

FLYING CAGE IN BIRD HOUSE

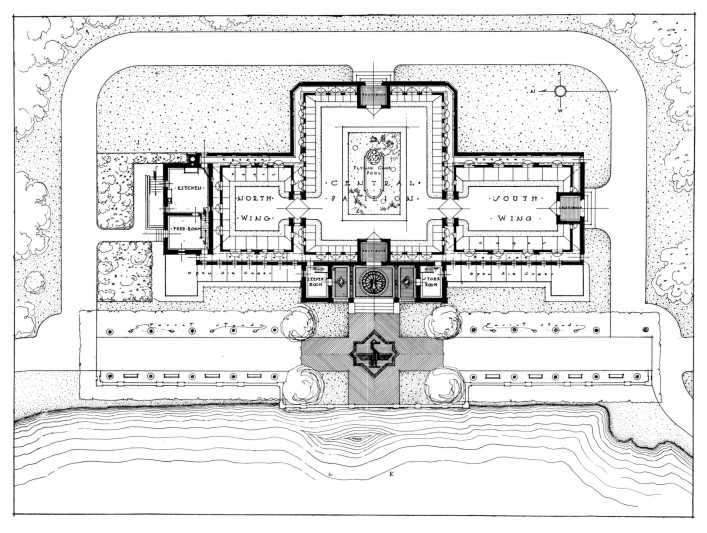

PLAN

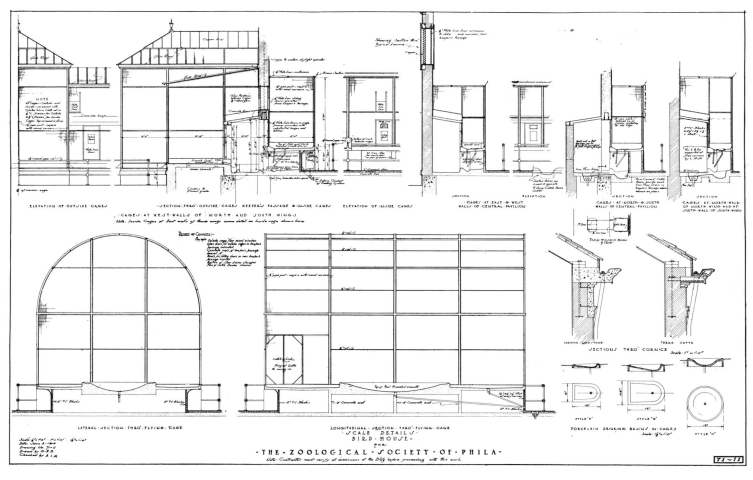

INTERIOR DETAILS

1915

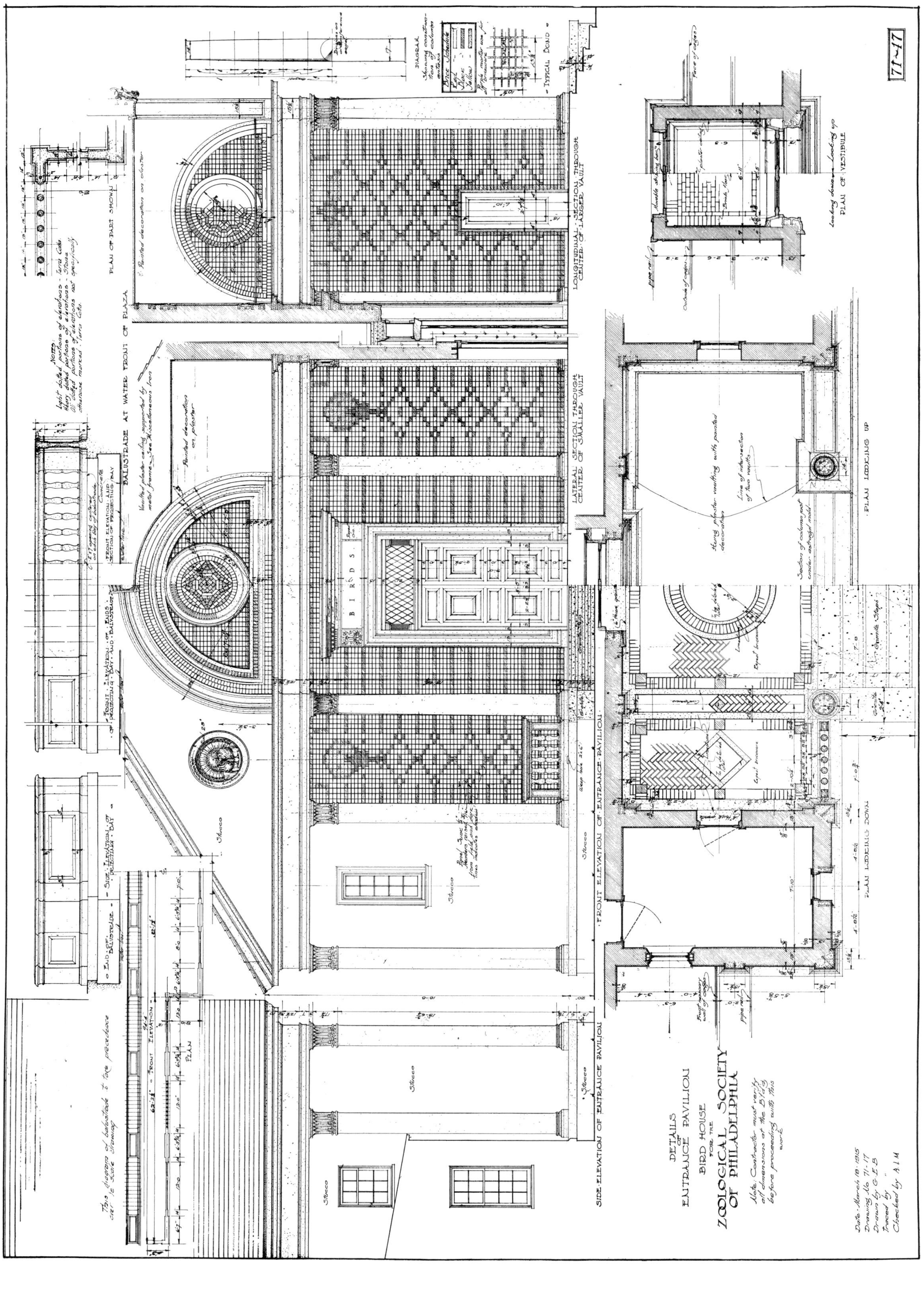

ENTRANCE PAVILION

THE FRONT

ORNAMENTAL IRON WORKSHOP FOR MR. SAMUEL YELLIN, PHILADELPHIA

1915

MAIN ENTRANCE GATE

WINDOW GRILLE

PRIVATE ENTRANCE GATE

GATE TO BACK YARD

COURT FROM VESTIBULE

CORNER OF BUILDING

FORGE ROOM

PRIVATE OFFICE

MUSEUM

COURT AND VESTIBULE

OUTSIDE STAIRWAY

THE BIG WINDOW

BIG WINDOW FROM WITHIN

ENTRANCE TO BIG ROOM

FIREPLACE END OF BIG ROOM

FROM THE LIBRARY GARDEN

DRAUGHTING ROOM

ENTRANCE

NORTH ROOM

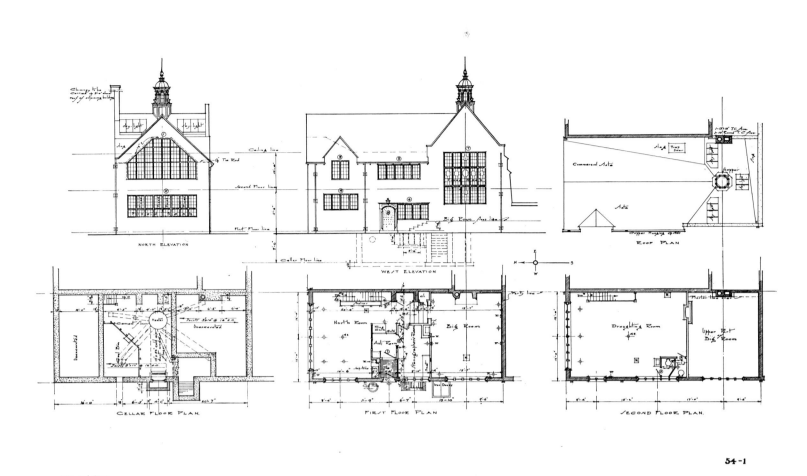

PLANS, ELEVATIONS AND DETAILS OF BIG ROOM

FARM BUILDINGS FOR MORRIS E. LEEDS, ESQ., CLONMELL, CHESTER COUNTY, PA.

1921

COW STABLE AND MILK HOUSE

FARM BUILDINGS FOR MORRIS E. LEEDS, ESQ., CLONMELL, CHESTER COUNTY, PA.

1921

GENERAL VIEW

IMPLEMENT SHED AND GARDEN

FARM BUILDINGS FOR MORRIS E. LEEDS, ESQ., CLONMELL, CHESTER COUNTY, PA.

1921

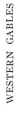

WESTERN GABLES

SILOS

FARM BUILDINGS FOR ALFRED MELLOR, ESQ., CUMMINGTON, MASS.

1916

TOWER AND MILK HOUSE

GENERAL VIEW

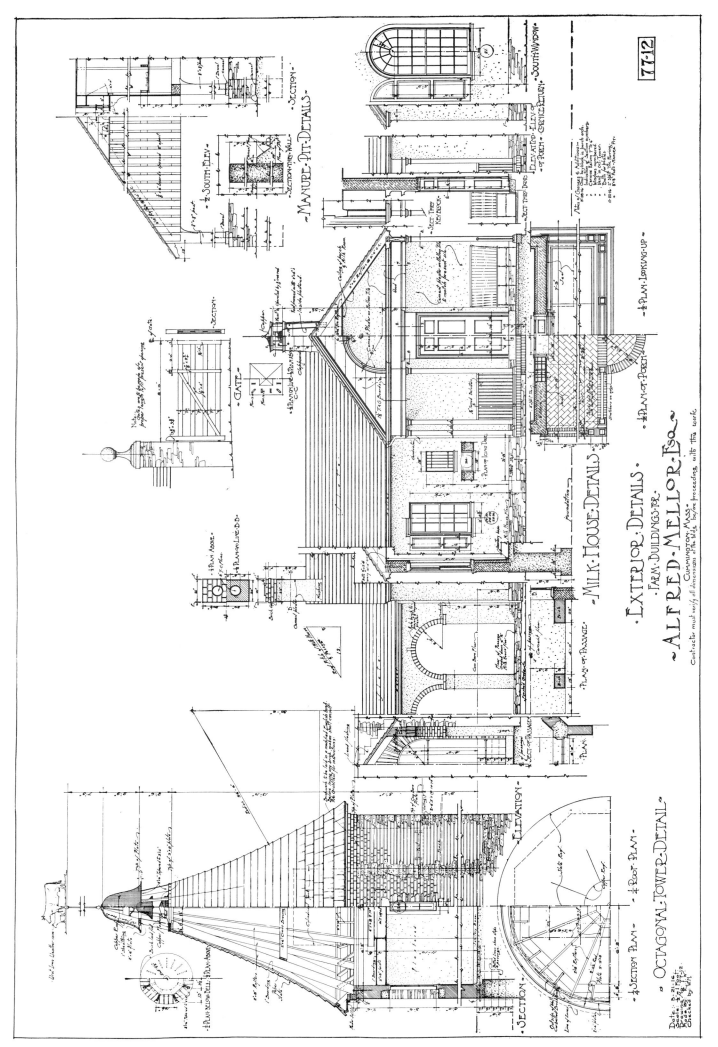

BARN AND POLO STABLE FOR A. J. DREXEL PAUL, ESQ., RADNOR, PA.

1913

GENERAL VIEW

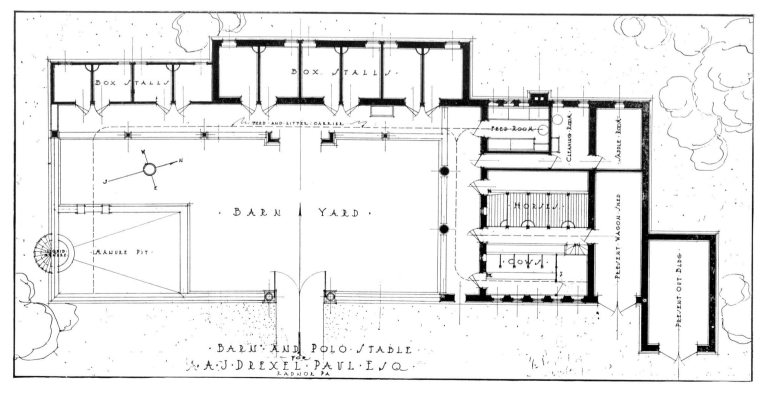

PLAN

The DEVELOPMENT of the ESTATE of ARTHUR E. NEWBOLD, Jr., Esq. LAVEROCK, PENNSYLVANIA

AN OLD-FASHIONED farm was brought into existence, with one main animating purpose, — the desire or necessity of making a living.

A modern farm is brought into existence with a different purpose, — the desire to make money.

Distinction between the two lies in the fact that the former was "general" in character, while the latter is "specialized." Little or nothing was brought from outside to an old-fashioned farm; little or nothing went from it, and the world around might cease while the farm continued, since it possessed all the essentials of life necessary to both man and beast. Everything was on it. Woods and streams and pastures, horses, cows, sheep and pigs; ducks and geese, turkeys and chickens; crops of wheat and hay and corn; all the vegetables, and all the fruits. And the great farming cycle went on. The horse cultivated the fields that produced the hay and the corn and the oats, and when ripe and harvested, the horse ate them, and gave back a tithe in the form of manure that went to produce more crops the following year. The cows and the sheep and the pigs fed from the same source, as did also the poultry, and they all were eaten by the man. Thus did an old-fashioned farm supply a living.

Not so with the modern specialized farm, designed to make money. Here there is only one thing produced, which has to be sent forth to the four corners of the earth to reach its market; while everything that is needed by those who live upon the land must be brought in from without. No farming cycle exists, for if it is a wheat farm, man cannot live by bread alone, nor would he be well if he lived on a diet composed only of fruit, in the event of his being the owner of an apple farm. All must come from without, while what is produced must be sent away, and after this transaction has taken place it is hoped that a money balance will appear in favor of the farmer, — which constitutes farming to make money.

The process of making a living out of a farm—that is out of the land—will, by its very essence, produce results resembling nature in their beauty, since the elements that are being dealt with are natural, and any organic arrangement of natural elements cannot fail to produce a beautiful whole; so that generations of farmers in the past have lived and toiled among lovely surroundings, being themselves as unconscious of the loveliness about them as birds and cattle are of their own forests and pastures; and these birds and cattle the farmers of the past greatly resembled, living as they did in a state of harmony and sympathy with their surroundings almost as complete as that of their own animals, and actually enhancing the beauty of the land which they inhabited as birds glorify a forest.

On the other hand, a farm that is designed to make money has all the ugliness of money-making in general. It has been found by experts that a cow tramples down three times as much grass as she eats; hence in the modern dairy farm, the cattle are kept in the barn, their food is brought to them and no more do they enhance the beauty of the landscape. In an apple farm, it has been found that after the young trees are well established, the weeds between the rows do no harm to the crop, so they are allowed to remain, and perhaps reproduce themselves upon other nearby farms, as is the habit of weeds. It matters not to this apple-grower, since his mind is occupied elsewhere. It is his hope that apple crops in all parts of the country, save his own, will fail, because only in that event can he hope to secure a ready market and a high price for what he has to sell. That he should feel this way is logical, having assumed the premise. He has the farm to make money—not a living—and only in this way can he make money.

It is not within the field of this discussion to inquire which is better and which is worse; the only answer sought is, —which do we like the best? We are all part of the same scheme of things; the humble men and women in Gray's "Elegy Written in a Country Churchyard," and Shakespeare's "Shylock;" but are we really to be forbidden from forming some sort of opinion of our own by those who tell us that "everything that is, has to be?"

The owner of this farm at Laverock does not depend entirely upon the products of his land for his livelihood, — the simple object sought being an effort to surround a pleasant country dwelling with some of the appurtenances that properly belong to country life, some of the elements above described that go with an old-fashioned farm, instead of living in a suburban villa that differs only from a house in town by being less advantageously situated.

The whole property comprises ninety acres, and is lived on by various members of the same family. There is a central farm group, not shown in the present presentation, from which the whole farm is operated, leaving the consideration of the sheep, the pigeons, the ducks and the geese, shown in the photographs, as a thing apart, to be especially enjoyed by this particular member of the family; and although it is recognized that the animals that live in the Farm Court and the vegetables that grow in the Potager do not constitute their owners only means of support, yet he uses them all as far as they will go—the important point being that they have been treated as a thing of beauty and delight, to be associated with on terms of intimacy as close as modern requirements will permit, and not relegated to an out of the way spot, as a thing to be kept hidden. What greater form of economy could be practiced than making something useful serve as a source of beauty, having reached the conviction that vegetables and animals are in themselves beautiful, and that, sympathetically handled, they supply, by their very presence, a never-ending source of beauty and enjoyment.

The house, which was not designed by this firm, is situated directly on the top of a high ridge of land running east and west, and when the present development was begun, it was without surroundings of any sort save the entrance road, and exposed to every winter wind that blows across the White Marsh Valley, which is below it and to the North.

An idea of this valley may be obtained from the cut entitled "Door to Northern World," while the frontispiece shows the slope of the land to the South. The wall that connects the house with the Belvedere was one of the earliest steps, being an effort to mitigate the severity of the Northwest winds that swept over the house like a ship at sea.

In this whole plan the focal point is the determination to bring the animals into close relation with the living part of the scheme, their habitation being so situated that it is necessary to pass directly through it to reach the house, and it was only after long consideration and reflection that this determination was reached. In France, or in fact throughout all older civilizations, one may find thousands of examples of "manoirs" and farms in which it is necessary to pass directly through the farm court to reach the house, which is, in fact, the main feature of the court, the front door opening directly upon it. In such cases, the animals are kept in by the house and farm buildings surrounding the court, and the main entrance gate has to be opened and closed and the court traversed, with its manure and mud, by anyone wishing to gain access to the house.

While such a scheme is perfect in its directness, it did not seem suitable for our modern requirements of cleanliness, and a solution was sought whereby the close association with animal life would be retained, while the disadvantages of the mud and manure, and the necessity of opening and closing the gate would be eliminated. Hence the present scheme, with its high wall around the northern part of the farm court (shown on page 201) pierced by its two openings and traversed by the main entrance drive.

The house, the high wall, and the sheep fold form the protection from the Northwest winds, and the Goose Pond forms the barrier which prevents the animals from straying from their own particular sphere; while from the drive, either in a motor or on foot, one feels that one has passed directly through and among the animals themselves.

The location of the sheep fold seems almost an absolute necessity, since it forms the main barrier and division between the living part of the scheme and the animals, with all its doors and functions to the East, and its garden side to the West (see Frontispiece and pages 200 and 204). Furthermore, the above considerations lead to an interesting architectural technicality. To obtain this object of separation, the long axis of the building had to run North and South and, as has already been described, the land slopes considerably towards the South—the level of the ground at the Pigeon Tower being five feet lower than the surface of the Goose Pond. Had the roof of the building run level throughout its entire length, it would not have fitted the ground on which it stood, and a ridge pole and eaves slanting down could not have been other than uneasy; so the whole plan of the building was curved, like a truncated plan of a ship—the curve being expressed in the ridge and, in fact, throughout the entire roof; as may be seen from all the photographs. The building is eighteen feet wide at the North, nineteen feet wide one-third of the way down, and sixteen feet wide at the Southernmost end. An extremely satisfactory impression of strength is imparted to the whole, very similar to the impression of strength produced by the curved lines of a ship, not only in its plan, but in the curved sections of its hull and of its decks as well—while in the case of this building it seems almost to cling to the land on which it stands.

In the matter of cost of construction, the difference between the curved plan and a straight one is negligible, since the only additional trouble involved is in laying out the foundations of the walls on a gentle curve, and the cutting of the rafters to a different length, while the pitch remains constant. Thus the curve of the plan is expressed in the ridge, and the whole surface of the roof becomes a curved plane.

The roof of the Pigeon Tower is again somewhat unusual, being constructed entirely of courses of brick laid in concentric rings. This method of spanning a space is, of course, very well known—each separate ring of brick laid header, arching itself, and thus becoming self-supporting;—but as is so often the case with accidental results, this particular roof seems admirably adapted to the roof of a Pigeon Tower, since it literally forms a "pigeon stairway." Each ring sets back about an inch and a half from the ring below it, and the pigeons light on it, and actually walk up it as if they were engaged in devotional exercises on the Scala Sancta.

The quoins and lintels about the openings in the Sheep Fold and Pigeon Tower are of concrete, the color of which closely approximates that of limestone. The lintels were cast in place, but all the quoins were cast on the ground in forms made by the carpenter of rough lumber at the beginning of building operations and the surface of the concrete was left untouched after the removal of the forms—a pleasant texture being thus easily obtained.

Passing from the Farm Court through the Potager to the Garden, the key changes in an ascending scale from animals to vegetables to flowers. The Potager is the main source of supply for all manner of vegetables and small fruits, some of the walks being bordered with box edging and some with strawberry vines, while at the corners of the beds are dwarf fruit trees with flowers between, and the large spaces contain the vegetables in rows, such as egg plants, artichokes, peas, lima beans, and so on through the large category of possibilities. The paths are of gravel, and all but the two main ones are, speaking technically, "two man" paths; that is, wide enough for two persons to walk abreast, while that on the main axis from the Cattle Pool to the central opening in the Pergola is eight feet wide on account of the important place it occupies in the design, and the path leading from the opening between the Sheep Fold and the Pigeon Tower to the Western end of the Potager is ten feet wide to enable a horse and cart to be driven through the Potager, turned in the field beyond, and brought back; a very necessary and convenient feature in the operation of a vegetable garden. The sheep which constantly gather at the gate separating the Farm Court from the Potager tell us very pleasantly that even in the Potager we are not far from our animals.

In the Cattle Pool we have again an excellent example of beauty growing out of necessity, for a pleasanter sight than cattle drinking is hard to find. These cows do not have to be driven up to this Pool, where they make such a lovely decorative feature to the whole Potager. They come there of their own accord, and when they come, they stay about— automatically. Again the Pool has another and an accidental use. Primarily it is for the cows, but for the owner's children it is too good to miss, so they swim in it, or rather flounder and splash in it, and they and the cows use this pool in a happy harmony; but not at the same time.

At one end of the Pergola is the Belvedere, which constitutes the only "porch," with its iron grilles and shutters, and at the other end is the Sun Trap and Fountain. As the names imply, one is for hot weather and the other is for cold, while they both command the same sweeping, northern view of the White Marsh Valley; and although this view is extensive, its northern quality makes it a little like a tiger—we prefer to look at it through a set of bars!

The circular brick Pavement to the north of the Belvedere is like the roof of an Arab house. As the two ends of the Pergola have been described as being arranged for hot weather and cold, so the two sides of the wall are for noontide and evening. A cheerless-looking spot it is in the middle of a hot summer day (like an Arab roof) with four or five chairs starkly staring at each other around a shadeless, brick ring under a scorching sun; but when the day's veil falls from the world of sleep, it draws one like a magnet—or like an Arab roof—situated as it is with one vast canopy over it, and that the sky.

If the ideas, merely sketched and hinted at in the beginning of this description, have in them any soundness whatever, if making money is, in its very essence, an uninspiring pursuit, if making a "living," or, as in this case—living—is capable of becoming extremely interesting; is it flying too much in the face of modern accepted thought, on progress (whatever that may be), on organization, specialization, efficiency—to attempt to cling to something that has almost gone out of our lives and, by mixing together in one whole, flowers, vegetables, animals, and children, to pray that some of that poetry, which constituted everyday life of past generations, may be brought back into our own?

ARTHUR I. MEIGS.

DEVELOPMENT OF ESTATE OF ARTHUR E. NEWBOLD, JR., ESQ., LAVEROCK, PA.

1922

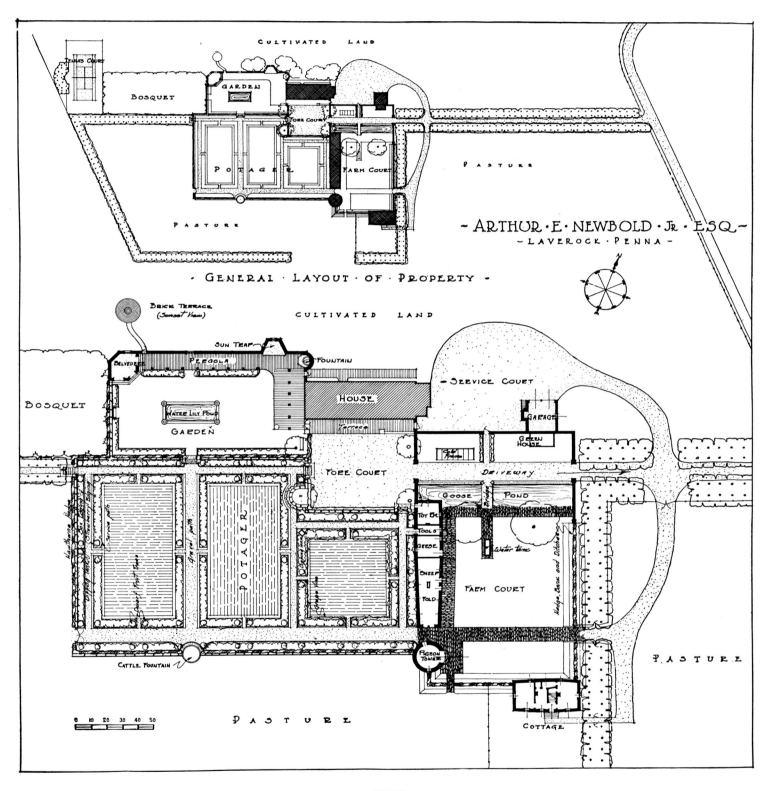

PLAN

DEVELOPMENT OF ESTATE OF ARTHUR E. NEWBOLD, JR., ESQ., LAVEROCK, PA.

1922

WEST SIDE OF SHEEP FOLD

DEVELOPMENT OF ESTATE OF ARTHUR E. NEWBOLD, JR., ESQ., LAVEROCK, PA.

1922

POTAGER

SUN TRAP

GARAGE FROM FORECOURT

DEVELOPMENT OF ESTATE OF ARTHUR E. NEWBOLD, JR., ESQ., LAVEROCK, PA.

1922

BELVEDERE

TERMINATION OF PERGOLA

DEVELOPMENT OF ESTATE OF ARTHUR E. NEWBOLD, JR., ESQ., LAVEROCK, PA.

1922

DOOR TO NORTHERN WORLD

COW POOL

DEVELOPMENT OF ESTATE OF ARTHUR E. NEWBOLD, JR., ESQ., LAVEROCK, PA.

1922

GOOSE POND

DEVELOPMENT OF ESTATE OF ARTHUR E. NEWBOLD, JR., ESQ., LAVEROCK, PA.

1922

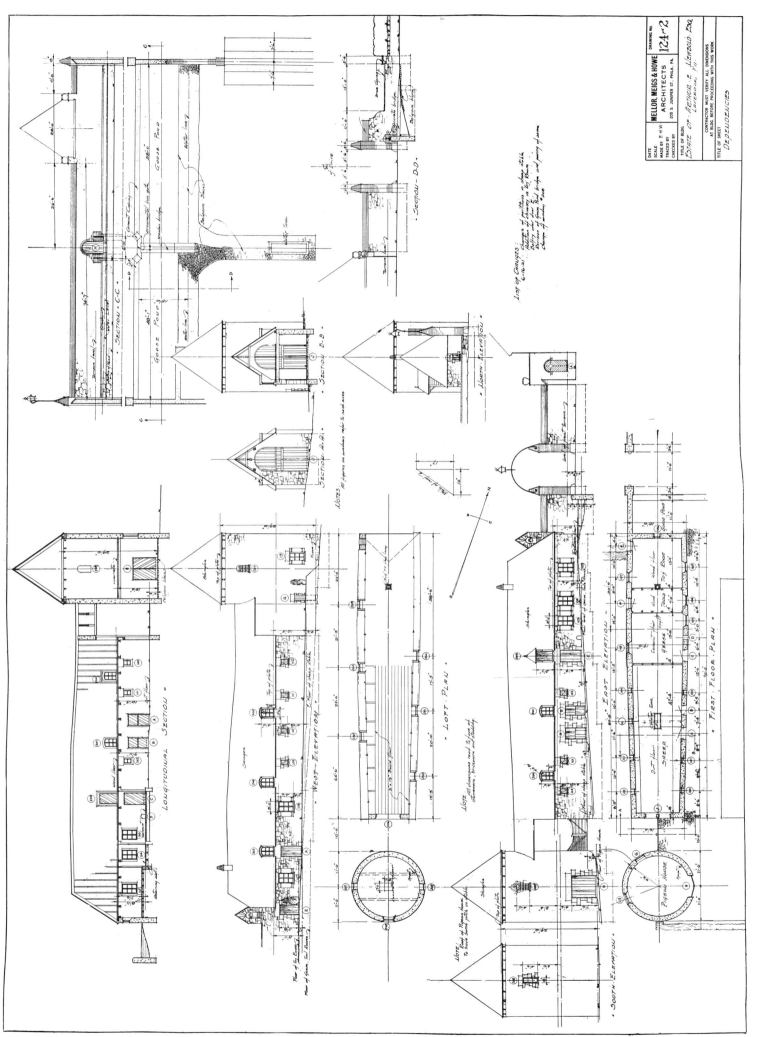

PLANS AND ELEVATIONS

DEVELOPMENT OF ESTATE OF ARTHUR E. NEWBOLD, JR., ESQ., LAVEROCK, PA.

1922

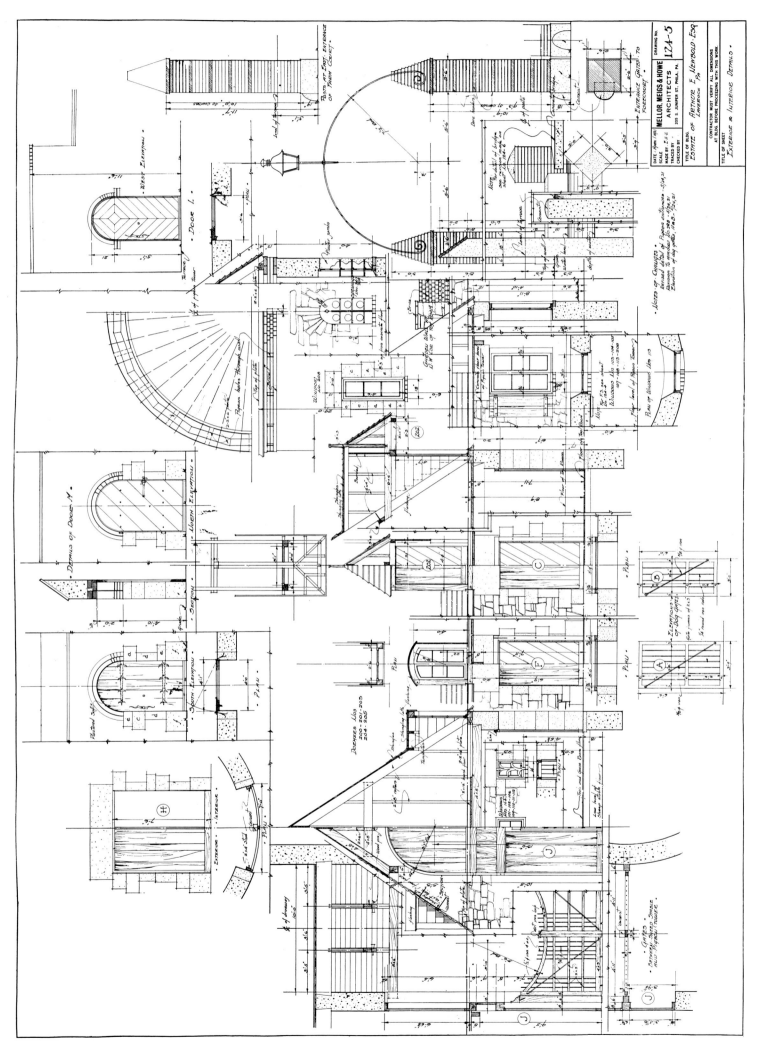

EXTERIOR DETAILS

DEVELOPMENT OF ESTATE OF ARTHUR E. NEWBOLD, JR., ESQ., LAVEROCK, PA.

1922

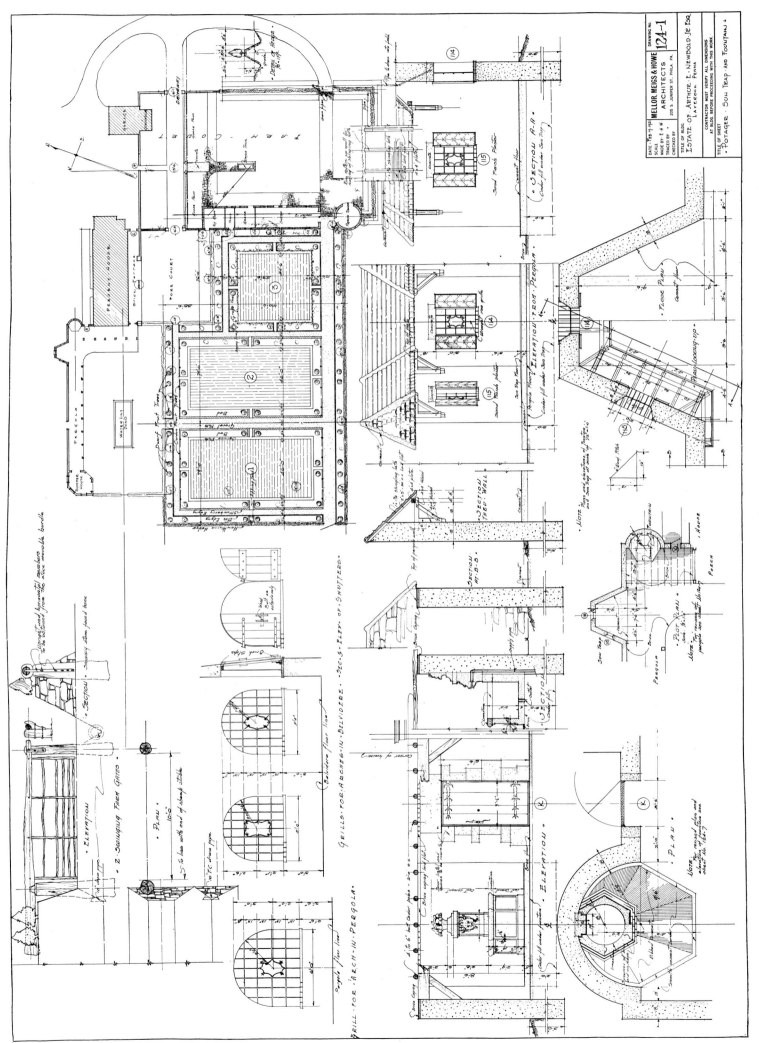

SUN TRAP AND POTAGER

HOUSE FOR C. W. MORRIS, ESQ., HAVERFORD, PA.

1915